Iran: U.S. Concerns and Policy Responses

IRAN: U.S. CONCERNS AND POLICY RESPONSES

KENNETH KATZMAN

Nova Science Publishers, Inc.
New York

LIBRARY OF CONGRESS CATALOGING-IN-PUBLICATION DATA

Iran : U.S. concerns and policy responses / Kenneth Katzman (editor).
p. cm.
Includes index.
ISBN 978-1-60456-845-5 (softcover)
1. United States--Foreign relations--Iran. 2. Iran--Foreign relations--United States. 3. United States--Foreign relations--2001- 4. Iran--Foreign relations--1997- I. Katzman, Kenneth.
E183.8.I55166 2008
327.73055--dc22

2008024211

Published by Nova Science Publishers, Inc. ≃ New York

CONTENTS

PREFACE

The Bush Administration has pursued several avenues to attempt to contain or end the potential threat posed by Iran, at times pursuing limited engagement, and at other times leaning toward pursuing efforts to change Iran's regime. Some experts believe a potential crisis is looming over Iran's nuclear program because the Bush Administration is skeptical that efforts by several European allies to prevent a nuclear breakout by Iran will succeed, although the Administration announced steps in March 2005 to support those talks. U.S. concerns have been heightened by the victory of Mahmoud Ahmadinejad, an admitted hardliner, in Iran's presidential election on June 24, 2005. Some advocate military action against Iran's nuclear infrastructure, but others believe that a combination of diplomatic and economic rewards and punishment are the only viable options on the nuclear issue. U.S. sanctions currently in effect ban or strictly limit U.S. trade, aid, and investment in Iran and penalize foreign firms that invest in Iran's energy sector, but unilateral U.S. sanctions do not appear to have materially slowed Iran's WMD programs to date.

Other major U.S. concerns include Iran's policy in the Near East region, particularly Iran's material support to groups that use violence against the U.S.-led Middle East peace process, including Hizballah in Lebanon and the Palestinian groups Hamas and Palestinian Islamic Jihad. Some senior Al Qaeda activists are in Iran as well, although Iran claims they are "in custody" and will be tried. Iran did not obstruct the U.S. effort to oust Iraq's Saddam Hussein, a longtime Tehran adversary, at least partly in the expectation that pro-Iranian Shiite Islamic factions would come to power in Iraq in the aftermath. That result occurred as a

product of January 30, 2005 elections there. Iran is also assisting pro-
Iranian local leaders in Afghanistan, although that support does not
appear to be materially hindering the stabilization and development of
Afghanistan.

Iran's human rights practices and strict limits on democracy have
been consistently criticized by official U.S. and U.N. reports, particularly
for Iran's suppression of political dissidents and religious and ethnic
minorities. New limits on personal freedoms could be imposed by
Ahmadinejad, who has consistently advocated a return to many of the
original principles of the Islamic revolution as set down by the late
Ayatollah Ruhollah Khomeini. However, Iran does hold elections for
some positions, including that of president, suggesting to some experts
that there might be benefits to engaging Iranian officials. According to
this view, new sanctions or military action could harden Iran's positions
without necessarily easing the potential threat posed by Iran.

Chapter 1

THREAT ASSESSMENTS AND U.S. CONCERNS

Much of the debate over U.S. policy toward Iran has centered on the nature of the current regime. Some experts believe that Iran is a threat to U.S. interests because hardliners in Iran's regime dominate and set a policy direction intended to challenge U.S. influence and allies in the region. The elements of that challenge include attempting to acquire weapons of mass destruction (WMD), supporting terrorist groups, and pressuring regional U.S. allies.

POLITICAL HISTORY

The United States was an ally of the late Shah of Iran, Mohammad Reza Pahlavi ("the Shah"), who ruled from 1941 until his ouster in February 1979. The Shah assumed the throne when Britain and Russia forced his father, Reza Shah Pahlavi (Reza Shah), from power because of his perceived alignment with Germany in World War II. Reza Shah had assumed power in 1921 when, as an officer in Iran's only military force, the Cossack Brigade, he launched a coup against the government of the Qajar Dynasty.

The Shah was anti-Communist, and the United States viewed his government as a bulwark against the expansion of Soviet influence in the Persian Gulf. In 1951, he appointed a popular nationalist parliamentarian, Dr. Mohammad Mossadeq, as Prime Minister. Mossadeq was widely considered left-leaning, and the United States was wary of his policies, which included his drive for nationalization of the oil industry. Mossadeq's followers began an uprising in August 1953 when the Shah tried to dismiss Mossadeq, and the Shah fled. The Shah was restored in a CIAsupported coup that year, and Mossadeq was arrested.

Source: Map Resources. Adapted by CRS (K Yancey 4/12/05).

Figure 1. Map of Iran.

The Shah tried to modernize Iran and orient it toward the West, but in so doing he also tried to limit the influence and freedoms of Iran's Shiite clergy. He exiled Ayatollah Ruhollah Khomeini in 1964 because of Khomeini's active opposition to the Shah, opposition based on the Shah's anti-clerical policies and what Khomeini alleged was the Shah's forfeiture of Iran's sovereignty to its patron, the United States. Khomeini settled in and taught in Najaf, Iraq, before going to France in 1978, from which he stoked the Islamic revolution. Mass demonstrations and guerrilla activity by pro-Khomeini forces, allied with a broad array of anti-Shah activists, caused the Shah's government to collapse in February 1979.

Khomeini returned from France and, on February 11, 1979, declared an Islamic Republic of Iran. The Islamic republic is characterized by direct participation in government by Shiite Islamic theologians, a principle known as *velayat-e-faqih* (rule by a supreme Islamic jurisprudent). Khomeini was strongly anti-West and particularly anti-U.S., and relations between the United States and the Islamic Republic turned hostile even before the November 4, 1979, seizure of the U.S. Embassy by pro-Khomeini radicals.

REGIME STABILITY, JUNE 2005 PRESIDENTIAL ELECTIONS, AND HUMAN RIGHTS

After about a decade as leader of the revolution, Ayatollah Khomeini died on June 3, 1989; his regime is now led by his clerical disciples. Upon Khomeini's death, one of those followers, Ayatollah Ali Khamene'i, then serving as president, was selected Supreme Leader by an "Assembly of Experts" (an elected body). The Assembly also has the power to amend Iran's constitution. Although Khamene'i had served as elected president since 1981 (re-elected in 1985), he lacks the unquestioned spiritual and political authority of Khomeini, but he appears to face no direct threats to his position. The Supreme Leader appoints heads of key institutions, such as the armed forces, and half of the twelve-member Council of Guardians,[1] a body that reviews legislation to ensure it conforms to Islamic law. The Council of Guardians reviews election candidates. Another unelected body dominated by conservatives is the Expediency Council, set up in 1988 to resolve legislative disagreements between the *Majles* (parliament) and the Council of Guardians. Using these levers of power, Khamene'i and his allies have largely constrained the influence of the reformers.

Mohammad Khatemi, Reformists, and Reformist Candidates

Outgoing president Mohammad Khatemi was first elected in May 1997, with 69% of the vote. He was re-elected in June 2001, with an even larger 77% of the vote, against nine conservative candidates. Khatemi remains popular by most accounts, but he is politically subordinate to the Supreme Leader. Khatemi is a mid-ranking cleric, one rank below Ayatollah. He served as Minister of Culture and Islamic Guidance in the early 1990s but was dismissed from that post in 1993 because of criticism that he was allowing Western cultural material to receive wider distribution in Iran. From his dismissal until his election in 1997, he was head of Iran's national library. Khatemi has served two consecutive terms and constitutionally could not run again for president in the June 2005 presidential election.

Khatemi derived key political support from reformist-oriented students, youths, and women. Journalists and other observers say these reformist segments have been increasingly defiant of the hardliners in their dress and other activities, although observers say there are not overt signs of political rebellion. Khatemi's supporters held about 70% of the 290 seats in the 2000-2004 Majles after their victory in the February 18, 2000 elections. However, pro-reform elements became disillusioned with Khatemi for his refusal to confront the hardliners. Dissatisfaction with the lack of major reform erupted in major student demonstrations in July 1999 in which four students were killed by regime security forces. On June 8, 2003, a time period marking the fourth anniversary of those riots, regime forces again suppressed pro-reform demonstrators. Some of the 2003 protesters called for Khatemi to resign for being ineffective. President Bush issued statements in support of the demonstrators, although then Secretary of State Powell said the protests represented a "family fight" within Iran in which the United States should not seek a role. Institutionally, Khatemi has been supported by reformist organizations (formal "parties" have not been approved) that tried but failed to elect a reformist in the June 2005 elections:

- The Islamic Iran Participation Front (IIPF). The most prominent and best organized pro-reform grouping, it is headed by

Khatemi's brother, Mohammad Reza Khatemi, who was a deputy speaker in the 2000-2004 Majles.

- The student-led Office for Consolidation and Unity. It has become critical of Khatemi for failing to challenge the hardliners. In mid- 2002, partly in response to criticism by this organization, Khatemi proposed new legislation that would strengthen the power of his office; it was passed by the Majles but blocked by the Council of Guardians.

- The Mojahedin of the Islamic Revolution organization (MIR). It is composed mainly of left-leaning Iranian figures who, during the 1980s, sought greater state control of the economy and export of Iran's Islamic revolution to other countries in the region.

- The Society of Combatant Clerics. A prominent member of this grouping is Mehdi Karrubi, who was speaker of the 2000-2004 Majles. Karrubi finished third in the June 17, 2005 first round of the elections.

- Another registered reformist candidate in the June elections, and one who has attracted large sympathetic crowds in 2005 appearances, is former education minister Mostafa Moin. He was initially disqualified for the vote by the Council of Guardians, but his candidacy was reinstated on review. He finished fifth.

- Vice President (and Minister of Sports) Mohsen Mehralizadeh was another pro-reform candidate. He was also initially disqualified but reinstated on review. He finished last.

The Hardliners, Rafsanjani, and Hardline Candidates

Hardliners (conservatives) are now aligned under a multi-organization umbrella called the Fundamentalists' Coordination Council (FCC). The hardliners generally want only gradual reform, but more importantly in the view of most experts, they want to keep major governing and economic institutions under the control of members of their faction. Although unpopular with many segments of the population, they have gained momentum since February 28, 2003, municipal elections, when reformists failed to turn out in large numbers and hardliners won most of the seats from Tehran.

The power struggle between Khatemi and the conservatives caused a crisis in the run-up to the February 20, 2004 Majles elections. The Council of Guardians disqualified about 3,600 mostly reformist candidates, including 87 members of the current Majles. Some were prominent, such as deputy speakers Mohammad Reza Khatemi and Behzad Nabavi. Khatemi's IIPF grouping boycotted the elections, but some reformist factions participated. As was widely predicted before the election, conservatives fared well and won a majority, about 155 out of the 290 Majles seats. Turnout was about 51%, according to the reformist-controlled Interior Ministry, signaling that Iranians did not necessarily answer the call of some reformists not to participate. (Conservative controlled media put the turnout at about 60%, while some reformists said turnout was only about 35%.) The United States, most European Union countries, and other governments criticized this election as unfair. Just before the elections, on February 12, 2004, the Senate passed by unanimous consent S.Res. 304, expressing the sense of the Senate that the United States should not support the elections and should advocate "democratic government" in Iran. After these elections, on February 24, 2004, President Bush said in a White House statement "I join many in Iran and around the world in condemning the Iranian regime's efforts to stifle freedom of speech. I am very disappointed."

On the tide of the conservative victories, the chairman of the Expediency Council, former two-term president (1989-1997) Akbar Hashemi-Rafsanjani, regained his former political prominence he held in the 1980s. He is considered the patron of many Majles conservatives, although he ran for president again in the June 2005 elections on a pro-business, pro-reform platform. He was constitutionally permitted to run because a third term would not have been consecutive with his previous two terms as president.

Rafsanjani had several conservative opponents, four of whom had ties to the Islamic Revolutionary Guard Corps (IRGC, see below). They included former Revolutionary Guard commander Mohsen Rezai (now Secretary-General of the Expediency Council); former state broadcasting head Ali Larijani; former Revolutionary Guard Air Force commander and police chief, Mohammad Baqer Qalibaf; and Tehran mayor Mahmood Ahmadinejad, who was formerly a commander in the Guard and the *Basij* (a volunteer paramilitary organization that enforces adherence to Islamic customs). In deference to their patron, Rafsanjani, two prominent hardliners did not run: former foreign minister Ali Akbar Velayati; and chief nuclear negotiator Hassan Ruhani. Other major figures in the conservative camp who did not run are former Labor Minister Ahmad Tavakkoli, leader of the "Builders of Islamic Iran" faction, a key bloc in the new Majles, as well as the new Majles speaker, Gholem Ali Haded-Adel.

The Candidate Field and Results/Mahmoud Ahmadinejad

On May 22, 2005, the Council of Guardians, as expected, significantly narrowed the field of candidates to 6 out of the 1,014 persons who registered for the election. (In the 2001 presidential election, the Council permitted to run only 10 out of the 814 registered candidates.) However, at Khamene'i's request, two reformist candidates were reinstated. One, Reza'i, dropped out voluntarily before the June 17 first round.

In the June 17, 2005 first round, turnout was about 63% (29.4 million votes out of 46.7 million eligible voters). If no candidate received more than 50%, there would be a run-off of the top two vote getters. The results were as follows:

- Rafsanjani 21% (moved on to run-off)
- Ahmadinejad 19.5% (moved on to run-off)
- Karrubi 17%
- Qalibaf 13.8%
- Moin 13.77%
- Larijani 5.9%
- Mehralizadeh 4.38%
- Reza'i (dropped out before election)

The first round results proved surprising; virtually no experts foresaw the emergence of Tehran Mayor Ahmadinejad. Ahmadinejad, who is about 49, campaigned as a "man of the people," the son of a blacksmith who continues to live in modest circumstances, who would promote the interests of the poor and return government to the principles of the Islamic revolution during the time of Ayatollah Khomeini. Reformists were disappointed at the relatively poor showing of Moin, who had been expected by many to finish at least second. Other hardliners were surprised at Ahmadinejad's showing: Larijani had the support of the largest hardline organizations and Qalibaf was considered somewhat popular for exercising restraint during his time as Tehran police chief. Karrubi and some others alleged fraud in the first round, and the Council of Guardians ordered a spot-check of at least 50 ballot boxes, but a consensus emerged that widespread fraud was unlikely and there was no full-scale investigation. On the eve of the first round, President Bush criticized the elections as unfair because of the denial of the candidacies of "popular reformers and women who have done so much for the cause of freedom and democracy in Iran."[2]

The run-off was conducted on June 24, 2005. With his momentum from the first round, Ahmadinejad won a landslide victory in the run-off, receiving 61.8% of the vote to Rafsanjani's 35.7%. Turnout was 47%, less than the first round, suggesting that reformists did not turn out in large numbers to try to prevent Ahmadinejad's election. He becomes the first non-cleric to be president of the Islamic republic since the assassination of then president Mohammad Ali Rajai in August 1981.

At a news conference after the election, Ahmadinejad appealed for unity and pledged to build a unity government that includes officials on the reformist side of the spectrum. He stated that he would continue the nuclear talks with the European countries (discussed below), although he is believed to lean toward the views of other hardliners that Iran should not bargain the nuclear program away in talks with the Europeans. In keeping with his skepticism of relations with the United States, he made no significant overtures to the United States. At the same time, Ahmadinejad will face the same constraints from the Supreme Leader and the unelected bodies discussed above that have been faced by Khatemi, and Ahmadinejad's ability to implement major shifts in Iran's foreign and defense policies are likely limited, if he envisions such changes.

Prominent Dissidents

Several major dissidents seek sweeping change. One dissident cleric, Ayatollah Hossein Ali Montazeri, was released in January 2003 from several years of house arrest. He had been Khomeini's designated successor until 1989, when Khomeini dismissed him for allegedly protecting intellectuals and other opponents of clerical rule. He has since remained under scrutiny by the regime, but in September 2003, he criticized the seizure of the U.S. Embassy in 1979 as well as the core principle of the revolution: direct participation in government by the clerics. Other prominent dissidents include exiled theoretician Abd al-Karim Soroush, former Interior Minister Abdollah Nuri, and political activist Hashem Aghajari (of the Mojahedin of the Islamic Revolution), who was initially sentenced to death for blasphemy but whose sentence was overturned; he has been released.

Anti-Regime Groups: People's Mojahedin Organization of Iran (PMOI)

Some groups in exile seek the outright replacement of the current regime with one that is nationalist, secular, or left-wing. One group, which is left-leaning, is the People's Mojahedin Organization of Iran (PMOI).[3] Even though it is an opponent of Tehran, since the late 1980s, the State Department has refused contact with the PMOI and its umbrella organization, the National Council of Resistance (NCR). The PMOI, formed in the 1960s to try to overthrow the Shah of Iran, advocated Marxism blended with Islamic tenets. It allied with pro-Khomeini forces during the Islamic revolution but was later excluded from power and forced into exile. The State Department designated the PMOI as a foreign terrorist organization (FTO) in October 1997[4] and the NCR was named as an alias of the PMOI in the October 1999 re-designation. On August 14, 2003, the State Department designated the NCR offices in the United States an alias of the PMOI and NCR and ordered those facilities closed. The FTO designation was prompted by PMOI attacks in Iran that sometimes killed or injured civilians — although the group does not appear to purposely target civilians — and by its alleged killing of seven American defense advisers to the former

Shah in 1975-1976. In November 2002, a letter signed by about 150 House Members was released, asking the President to remove the PMOI from the FTO list.[5]

U.S. forces attacked PMOI military installations in Iraq during Operation Iraqi Freedom and negotiated a ceasefire with PMOI military elements in Iraq, requiring the approximately 4,000 PMOI fighters to remain confined to their Ashraf camp near the border with Iran. The group's weaponry is in storage, guarded by U.S. military personnel. Press reports continue to say that some Administration officials want the group removed from the FTO list and want a U.S. alliance with the group against the Tehran regime.[6] Then National Security Adviser Condoleezza Rice appeared to resolve that debate in November 2003 when she said that the United States is unambiguously treating the group as a terrorist organization. However, the debate over the group was renewed with the U.S. decision in late July 2004 to grant the Ashraf detainees "protected persons" status under the 4th Geneva Convention, meaning they will not be extradited to Tehran or forcibly expelled as long as U.S. forces remain in Iraq. The PMOI has used this determination to argue that the group should no longer be designated as an FTO. In other action against the group, on June 17, 2003, France arrested about 170 PMOI members, including its co-leader Maryam Rajavi (wife of PMOI founder Masoud Rajavi, who is still based in Iraq.) She was subsequently released and remains in France.[7]

Pro-Shah Activists/Exile Broadcasts

Some Iranian exiles, as well as some in Iran, want to replace the regime with a constitutional monarchy presumably led by the U.S.-based son of the late former Shah. On January 24, 2001, the Shah's son, Reza Pahlavi, who is about 54 years old, ended a long period of inactivity by giving a speech in Washington D.C. calling for unity in opposition to the current regime as well as the institution of a constitutional monarchy and genuine democracy in Iran. He has since broadcast messages into Iran from Iranian exile-run stations in California, and press reports say a growing number of Iranians inside Iran are listening to his broadcasts, although he is not believed to have a large following there.[8] Numerous other Iranian exile broadcasts, some not linked to the Shah's son, emanate from California, where there is a large Iranian-American community, but no U.S. assistance is provided to these stations. Then deputy Secretary of State Armitage testified before the Senate Foreign Relations Committee on October 28, 2003, that following a request to the Cuban government, the jamming from Cuba of Iranian exile and U.S. broadcasting to Iran had ceased; the jamming was carried out by Iranians in Cuba, not the Cuban government, according to Armitage.

Human Rights Record/Crackdowns on Dissent

U.S. officials have not generally considered Iran's human rights record as a strategic threat to U.S. interests, but the Administration has strongly criticized Iran's human rights record as part of its effort to pressure Iran. A special U.N. Human Rights Commission monitoring mission for Iran, consisting of reports by a "Special Representative" on Iran's human rights record, was conducted during 1984-2002. Iran has since agreed to "thematic" monitoring consisting of periodic U.N. investigations of specific aspects of Iran's human rights record. Iran is a party to the two international covenants on human rights. According to testimony on May 19, 2005, by Undersecretary of State for Political Affairs Nicholas Burns, the Bush Administration has established with European allies and Canada a "Human Rights Working Group" on Iran that will meet quarterly to coordinate how to spotlight and curb Iran's human rights abuses.

The United States continues to closely scrutinize Iran's human rights record. State Department's human rights report for 2004, released February 28, 2005, said Iran's already poor human rights record "worsened" during the year.[9] The U.S. and U.N. human rights reports cite Iran for widespread human rights abuses (especially of the Baha'i faith), including summary executions, disappearances, torture, and arbitrary arrest and detention. Since 2000, hardliners in the judiciary have closed hundreds of reformist newspapers, although many have tended to reopen under new names, and authorities have imprisoned or questioned several editors and even some members of the Majles. Press reports from November 2004 say Iran has also begun blocking hundreds of pro-reform websites.

Among major specific themes and cases:

- There was an apparent beating death of a Canadian journalist of Iranian origin,Zahra Kazemi, while she was in Iranian detention. She had been detained in early July 2003 for filming outside Tehran's Evin prison. The trial of an intelligence agent who allegedly conducted the beating resulted in an acquittal on July 25, 2004, prompting widespread accusations that the investigation and trial were not fair. In April 2005, Iran rebuffed a Canadian attempt to conduct a formal autopsy of Kazemi.

- Iran's hardliners significantly downplayed the naming in October 2003 of Iranian human rights/women's rights lawyer Shirin Ebadi as winner of the Nobel Peace prize. In January 2005, a revolutionary court ordered her to appear; she refused, and the court then backed down and claimed its summons was an error.

- On May 13, 2005, Iran freed a prominent dissident, Abbas Abdi, who was jailed for the past two years for conducting an opinion poll on Iranians' attitudes toward relations with the United States.

- On the issue of women's rights, on June 13, 2005, about 250 women staged the first women's rights demonstration since the 1979 Islamic revolution, protesting obligatory veiling, the denial of their candidacies in the June 2005 presidential elections, and related practices. On the other hand, women can vote and run in lower level elections, including the Majles, they can drive, and many work outside the home, including owning and running their own businesses. Eleven out of the 290 Majles deputies are women. These rights mean that women are freer than in some nearby states such as Saudi Arabia.

- U.S. reports and officials continue to cite Iran for religious persecution. Since March 1999, the State Department has named Iran as a "Country of Particular Concern," each year under the International Religious Freedom Act, and no improvement in Iran's practices on this issue was noted in the International Religious Freedom report for 2004, released September 15, 2004. No sanctions have been added because of this designation, on the grounds that Iran is already subject to extensive U.S. sanctions.

- Iran is repeatedly cited for repression of the Baha'i community, which Iran's Shiite Muslim clergy views as a heretical sect. Two CRS-9 Baha'is (Dhabihullah Mahrami and Musa Talibi) were sentenced to death in 1996 for apostasy. On July 21, 1998, Iran executed Ruhollah Ruhani, the first Bahai executed since 1992 (Bahman Samandari). In February 2000, Iran's Supreme Court set aside the death sentences against three other Baha'is. Several congressional resolutions have condemned Iran's treatment of the Baha'is, including S.Con.Res. 57 (106th Congress), which passed the Senate July 19, 2000, and H.Con.Res. 257, which passed the House on September 19, 2000. In the 108th Congress, a proposed H.Con.Res. 319 contained a sense of Congress on the Baha'is similar to that in previous years.

- On the treatment of Jews, the 30,000-member Jewish community (the largest in the Middle East aside from Israel) enjoys more freedoms than Jewish communities in several other Muslim states. However, during 1993-1998, Iran executed five Jews allegedly spying for Israel. In June 1999, Iran arrested 13 Jews (mostly teachers, shopkeepers, and butchers) from the Shiraz area that it said were part of an "espionage ring" for Israel. After an April - June 2000 trial, ten of the Jews and two Muslims accomplices were convicted (July 1, 2000), receiving sentences ranging from 4 to 13 years. A three-judge appeals panel reduced the sentences, and the releases began in January 2001; the last five were freed in April 2003.

IRAN'S STRATEGIC CAPABILITIES AND WEAPONS OF MASS DESTRUCTION PROGRAMS

For the past two decades, the United States has sought to contain the strategic threat posed by Iran's WMD programs. Iran is not considered a major conventional threat to the United States, but some of its weapons of mass destruction (WMD) programs, particularly its nuclear and ballistic missile programs, have made significant progress and could potentially put U.S. allies and forces at risk.

Iran's armed forces total about 550,000 personnel, including both the regular military and the Revolutionary Guard. The latter is generally loyal to the hardliners and, according to some recent analysis, is becoming more assertive in political decisions as government leaders have become more dependent on it to maintain control. In mid-2004, Guard personnel closed part of a new airport in Tehran when the government chose a foreign (Turkish) contractor to run the airport.

Iran's ground forces are likely sufficient to deter or fend off conventional threats from Iran's relatively weak neighbors such as post-war Iraq, Turkmenistan, Azerbaijan, and Afghanistan. Iran has avoided cause for conflict with its more militarily capable neighbors such as Turkey and Pakistan. In February and March 2005, Commander of U.S. Central Command Gen. John Abizaid and head of the Defense Intelligence Agency Vice Admiral Lowell Jacoby both said that Iran has recently acquired some new capability (indigenously produced anti-ship missiles, and North Korean-supplied torpedo and missile boats) to block the Strait of Hormuz at the entrance to the Persian Gulf briefly, or to threaten the flow of oil through that waterway.[10] However, Iran is largely lacking in logistical ability to project power much beyond its borders. No major military tensions are currently evident between Iran and U.S. military forces in the Persian Gulf region, and U.S. military officials say that their encounters with Iranian naval vessels in the Gulf are mostly professional.

Iran's conventional capabilities have concerned successive U.S. Administrations far less than have Iran's attempts to acquire WMD. Partly because of recent acceleration of some of Iran's WMD programs, particularly its nuclear program, President Bush, in his January 29, 2002 State of the Union message, labeled Iran part of an "axis of evil" along with Iraq and North Korea.

Iran — and virtually all Iranian factions appear to agree on the utility of WMD — appears to see WMD, particularly the acquisition of a nuclear weapons capability, as a means of ending its perceived historic vulnerability to U.S. domination, or as a symbol of Iran's perception of itself as a major nation. Some see Iran's WMD programs as an instrument for Iran to dominate the Persian Gulf region. There are also fears Iran might transfer WMD to some of the extremist groups it supports, such as Lebanese Hizbollah, although there is no evidence to date that Iran has taken any steps in that direction. Iran's programs continue to be assisted primarily by entities in Russia, China, and North Korea.[11]

Nuclear Program[12]

Some observers believe a crisis between Iran and the international community over Iran's perceived nuclear ambitions is likely. As U.S. and European concerns about the scope of Iran's nuclear program have grown, U.S. and European policies have converged. The Bush Administration has supported an effort by France, Britain, and Germany (the "EU-3") to negotiate curbs on Iran's program. At the same time, the Administration is uncertain that the EU-3 approach will succeed. The Bush Administration and the U.S. intelligence community[13] assert that Iran is determined to achieve a nuclear weapons capability and that Iran, despite insisting its nuclear program is for only peaceful purposes, has not upheld its obligations under the 1968 Nuclear Non-Proliferation Treaty (NPT). On June 18, 2003, President Bush was quoted by press reports as stating that the United States would "not tolerate construction" of a nuclear weapon by Iran. Iranian leaders, including president-elect Ahmadinejad, say uranium enrichment is allowed under the NPT and that Iran will not give up the "right" to enrich uranium.

There is disagreement over the urgency of the issue. IAEA director Mohammad El Baradei continues to assert that the IAEA has not concluded Iran is trying to develop a nuclear weapon, although the IAEA said in November 2003 that Iran had failed to meet its reporting obligations under its Safeguards agreement with the IAEA. In testimony before the Senate Intelligence Committee on February 16, 2005, DIA head Adm. Jacoby (see above) said that, "Unless constrained by a nuclear nonproliferation agreement, Tehran probably will have the ability to produce nuclear weapons early in the next decade." However, Israeli experts are said to believe that Iran might reach "the point of no return," the point at which Iran would have the technical capability to construct a nuclear weapon, later in 2005.[14]

The international suspicions of Iran's intentions gained urgency in December 2002, when Iran confirmed PMOI allegations that it was building two additional facilities, at Arak and Natanz, that could be used to produce fissile material that could be used for a nuclear weapon. (Natanz could produce enriched uranium and the Arak facility reportedly is a heavy water production plant; heavy water is used in a reactor that is considered ideal for the production of plutonium.) Iran aggravated international concerns during most of 2003 by refusing to sign the "Additional Protocol" to the NPT, which would allow for enhanced inspections. (Iran did modify its Safeguards agreement to provide advanced notice of new nuclear facilities construction.) It was also revealed in 2003 that the founder of Pakistan's nuclear weapons program, Abdul Qadeer (A.Q.) Khan, sold Iran and other countries (Libya, North Korea) nuclear technology and designs. In March 2005, Pakistani officials said that Khan had provided unauthorized assistance, including centrifuges that could be used to enrich uranium, to Iran during the 1980s.[15] In February 2004, Khan publicly admitted selling nuclear technology to Iran, Libya, and North Korea.

At the same time, Russia, despite its own growing concerns about Iran's intentions, continued work on an $800 million nuclear power plant at Bushehr, under a January 1995 contract. Russia's Federal Atomic Energy Agency said in October 2004 that the reactor was essentially complete, but Russia insisted that Iran sign an agreement under which Russia would provide reprocess the plant's spent nuclear material; after many delays, that agreement was signed on February 28, 2005. The power plant, expected to become operational later in 2005 when Russia begins delivering fuel to it, could give Iran additional technologies for a weapons program (plutonium, for example), but the Russia-Iran reprocessing deal also adds safeguards that could slow an Iranian weapons program.

European Diplomatic Efforts/Agreement One

Believing that engagement might yield progress, beginning in 2003, the foreign ministers of Germany, France, and Britain (the "EU-3") undertook diplomacy to limit Iran's nuclear program. On October 21, 2003, the EU-3 and Iran issued a joint statement in which Iran pledged, in return for promises of future exports of peaceful nuclear technology, to fully disclose all aspects of its past nuclear activities; to sign and ratify the Additional Protocol; and to temporarily suspend uranium enrichment activities. Iran signed the Additional Protocol on December 18, 2003, and the IAEA says Iran is largely abiding by its provisions, although the Majles has not yet ratified it. However, the agreement deteriorated as it became clear that the international community would maintain strict scrutiny of Iran. Iran particularly objected to the findings of the November 10, 2003 and February 24, 2004 IAEA reports that Iran had committed violations of its obligations over an 18-year period; that traces of both highly enriched and low-enriched uranium had been found at two sites in Iran;[16] and that the Iranian military had been involved in manufacturing centrifuge equipment. In July 2004 Iran broke the IAEA's seals on some of its nuclear centrifuges, essentially scuttling the deal.

Subsequently, the IAEA said in September 2004 that Iran was preparing to convert 37 tons of uranium ("yellowcake") into uranium tetraflouride gas as a step toward making enriched uranium.[17] (In May 2005, Iran confirmed that it had done that conversion.) The breakdown of the 2003 agreement caused the Bush Administration to argue for referring the issue to the U.N. Security Council for the possible imposition of international sanctions.

European Diplomatic Efforts/Agreement Two

In the run-up to a November 25, 2004, IAEA board meeting that was potentially going to decide on a Security Council referral, the EU-3 sought Bush Administration backing for another diplomatic overture to Iran. The EU-3 held out for Iran a possible "grand bargain" in which Iran would forgo uranium enrichment in exchange for broad diplomatic engagement with Iran (resumed talks on an Iran-EU trade agreement, support for Iran's entry into the World Trade Organization, and counter-narcotics assistance) and assistance to the purely peaceful aspects of Iran's nuclear program (heavy water reactor, nuclear fuel).[18] The EU-3 conditioned the talks on Iran's suspension of all uranium enrichment activity, pending the reaching of the broad, permanent agreement. On November 14, 2004, Iran appeared to meet most European demands by agreeing to a rapid (as of November 22), verifiable suspension of uranium enrichment, to remain in place until a permanent agreement is reached. An IAEA board resolution, adopted November 28, 2004, did not threaten to refer the issue to the Security Council.

Since then, there have been some accusations that Iran is not complying with its terms. According to the Administration and the IAEA, Iran has limited IAEA access to two secret Iranian military sites, including the large Parchin complex, where suspected nuclear access might be taking place. IAEA inspectors visited the site in January 2005, but Iran has not allowed visits subsequently. Iran is also alleged to have withheld information and conducted maintenance and other work on centrifuge equipment and uranium conversion activities. It is also beginning construction of a heavy water research reactor, which would be well suited to plutonium production. Concluding its meeting on March 2, 2005, the IAEA issued a statement that was less critical of Iran than previous IAEA statements or resolutions, but called on Iran to provide pro-active cooperation. IAEA deputy chief Pierre Goldschmidt said on June 15, 2005, that Iran had recently admitted to experimenting with producing plutonium in 1998, five years later than Iran had previously acknowledged, constituting an additional breach of Iran's NPT obligations.

Status of the Talks

EU-3 - Iran negotiations on a permanent nuclear agreement formally began on December 13, 2004 and continued in Geneva in March 2005. (Related EU-Iran talks on a trade and cooperation accord began in January 2005. The EU-3 nuclear talks also include "working groups" discussing "security" issues and economic cooperation.) On March 11, 2005, the Administration announced it would support the European talks with Iran (see below) by offering some economic incentives to Iran. The incentives included dropping U.S. objections to Iran's application to the World Trade Organization, WTO) and facilitating sales of U.S. civilian aircraft parts to Iran. The Administration decided not to actually join the talks. It did drop its opposition to Iran's WTO application in late May 2005, paving the way for Iran to begin accession talks.

President-elect Ahmadinejad has said he will continue the talks and that the Iranian negotiating team will remain the same. However, before the elections, Iranian negotiator Hassan Ruhani said Iran might withdraw from the talks because the EU-3 has not accepted an Iranian proposal, discussed at the latest meetings in Geneva on April 19 and then in

London on April 29, that Iran be allowed to ultimately retain a research uranium enrichment capability (3,000 centrifuges). The United States is said to believe that Iran could use even a small enrichment program to work toward a nuclear weapons capability, and neither the United States nor the EU-3 are likely to accept that Iranian idea. Another Iranian proposal, that the West provide Iran with up to 10 nuclear power reactors, is also unlikely to be accepted. On May 13, 2005, the EU-3 wrote to Rouhani threatening that if Iran followed through on threats to resume uranium conversion activities, in contravention of its pledges, they would support a referral of the matter to the Security Council. A ministerial level meeting in Geneva on May 25 salvaged the talks, at least for now; it resulted in an agreement for the EU-3 to present Iran, by late July 2005, with a roadmap to achieve the permanent agreement under discussion. Iran, perhaps backing down in the face of a unified U.S. and EU-3 position, has said it would continue its freeze on uranium enrichment and reprocessing activities at least until then.

Chemical and Biological Weapons

Official U.S. reports and testimony, particularly the semi-annual CIA reports to Congress on WMD acquisitions worldwide, continue to state that Iran is seeking a self-sufficient chemical weapons (CW) infrastructure, and that it "may have already" stockpiled blister, blood, choking, and nerve agents — and the bombs and shells to deliver them. This raises questions about Iran's compliance with its obligations under the Chemical Weapons Convention (CWC), which Iran signed on January 13, 1993, and ratified on June 8, 1997. Recent CIA reports to Congress say Iran "probably maintain[s] an offensive [biological weapons] BW program... and probably has the capability to produce at least small quantities of BW agents.[19]

Missiles[20]

Largely with foreign help, Iran is becoming self sufficient in the production of ballistic missiles.

- *Shahab-3*. Two of its first three tests of the 800-mile range *Shahab- 3* (July 1998, July 2000, and September 2000) reportedly were inconclusive or unsuccessful, but Iran conducted an apparently successful series of tests in June 2003. Iran subsequently called the Shahab-3, which would be capable of hitting Israel, operational and in production, and Iran formally delivered several of them to the Revolutionary Guard. Iran publicly displayed six *Shahab-3* missiles in a parade on September 22, 2003. Despite Iran's claims, U.S. experts say the missile is not completely reliable, and Iran tested a "new" [purportedly more accurate] version of it on August 12, 2004. Iran called the test successful, although some observers said Iran detonated the missile in mid-flight, raising questions about the success of the test. On November 17, 2004, then Secretary of State Powell said there is some information that Iran might be working to adapt that missile to carry a nuclear warhead.[21]

- *Shahab-4*. In October 2004, Iran announced it had succeeded in extending the range of the Shahab-3 to 1,200 miles, and it added in early November 2004 that it is capable of "mass producing" this longer-range missile, which Iran calls the Shahab-4. If Iran has made this missile operational with the capabilities Iran claims, large portions of the Near East and Southeastern Europe would be in range, including U.S. bases in Turkey. Iran's new claims would appear to represent an abrogation of its pledge in November 7, 2003, to abandon development of a 1,200 mile range missile. On May 31, 2005, Iran announced it had successfully tested a solid-fuel version of the Shahab-3. The PMOI asserts Iran is secretly developing an even longer range missile, 1,500 miles, with the help of North Korean scientists.[22]

- *ICBM*. Iran's asserted progress on missiles would appear to reinforce the concerns of the U.S. intelligence community. In February 2005, DIA Director Jacoby testified that Iran might be capable of developing an intercontinental ballistic missile by 2015,[23] but that it was not yet clear whether Iran has decided to field such a system.

- *Other Missiles*. On September 6, 2002, Iran said it successfully tested a 200 mile range "Fateh 110" missile (solid propellent), and Iran said in late September 2002 that it had begun production of the missile.[24] On March 18, 2005, the *London Financial Times* reported that Ukraine has admitting 12 "X-55" cruise missiles to Iran in 2001; the missiles are said to have a range of about 1,800 miles. Iran also possesses a few hundred short-range ballistic missiles, including the *Shahab-1* (Scud-b), the *Shahab-2* (Scud-C), and the *Tondar-69* (CSS-8).

FOREIGN POLICY AND SUPPORT FOR TERRORISM

Iran's support for terrorist groups has long concerned U.S. Administrations, particularly since doing so gives Tehran an opportunity to try to obstruct the U.S.-led Middle East peace process. Tehran contends that the Arab-Israeli peace process is inherently weighted toward Israel, a U.S. ally, and cannot result in a fair outcome for the Palestinians. The State Department report on international terrorism for 2004, released April 23, 2005, again stated, as it has for most of the past decade, that Iran "remained the most active state sponsor of terrorism in 2004," although the report again attributes the terrorist activity to two hardline institutions: the Revolutionary Guard and the Intelligence Ministry.[25] Iran has been repeatedly accused of providing funding, weapons, and training to Hamas, Palestinian Islamic Jihad, Hizbollah, and the Popular Front for the Liberation of Palestine-General Command (PFLP-GC). In addition to these terrorist groups, the new report adds a non-Islamist Palestinian group: the Al Aqsa Martyr's Brigades. (All are named as foreign terrorist organizations (FTO) by the State Department.) Some other reports say that Iranian hardline factions have launched new recruiting drives in Iran and elsewhere, including in Africa, for potential terrorists.[26]

Analysts see Iran's support for terrorist groups as one element in a broader foreign policy.[27] Its policy is a product of the ideology of Iran's Islamic revolution, blended with and sometimes tempered by longstanding national interests that predate the Islamic revolution. Iran has tried to establish relatively normal relations with most of its neighbors, but, in its relations with some neighbors it has tried to actively influence internal events by promoting minority or anti-establishment factions.

Persian Gulf States[28]

During the 1980s and early 1990s, according to U.S. officials and outside experts, Iran sponsored Shiite Muslim extremist groups opposed to the monarchy states of the 6-member Gulf Cooperation Council (GCC; Saudi Arabia, Kuwait, Bahrain, Qatar, Oman, and the United Arab Emirates). These activities appeared to represent an effort by Iran to structure the Gulf region to its advantage by "exporting" its Islamic revolution. However, Iran's efforts were unsuccessful, and led the Gulf states to ally closely with the United States to confront Iran. By the mid-1990s, Iran began to shift more away from confrontation with the Gulf states by ending support for Shiite dissident movements there, a shift that accelerated after the election of Khatemi. Some believe it possible that presidentelect Ahmadinejad, who is associated with the Revolutionary Guard and other hardline institutions, might shift to the earlier stance of attempting to intimidate the Gulf states.

- *Saudi Arabia.* Many observers closely watch the relationship between Iran and Saudi Arabia as an indicator of Iran's overall posture in the Gulf. During the 1980s, Iran sponsored disruptive demonstrations at annual Hajj pilgrimages in Mecca, some of which were violent, and Iran sponsored Saudi Shiite dissident movements. Iran and Saudi Arabia restored relations in December 1991 (after a four-year break), and progressed to high-level contacts during Khatemi's presidency. In May 1999, Khatemi became the first senior Iranian leader to visit Saudi Arabia since the Islamic revolution; he visited again on September 11, 2002. (Supreme Leader Khamene'i has been invited to as well but has not done so.) The exchanges suggest that Saudi Arabia has tried to move beyond the issue of the June 25, 1996, Khobar Towers housing complex bombing, which killed 19 U.S. airmen, and was believed by some to have been orchestrated by Iranian agents.[29]
- The United Arab Emirates (UAE) has considered the Islamic regime of Iran aggressive since April 1992, when Iran asserted complete control of the Persian Gulf island of Abu Musa, which it and the UAE shared under a 1971 bilateral agreement. (In 1971, Iran, then ruled by the U.S.-backed Shah, seized two other

islands, Greater and Lesser Tunb, from the emirate of Ras al-Khaymah, as well as part of Abu Musa from the emirate of Sharjah.) The UAE wants to refer the dispute to the International Court of Justice (ICJ), but Iran insists on resolving the issue bilaterally. In concert with Iran's reduction of support for Gulf dissident movements, the UAE has not pressed the issue vigorously in several years, although the UAE still insists the islands dispute be kept on the agenda of the U.N. Security Council (which it has been since December 1971). The United States, which is concerned about Iran's military control over the islands, supports UAE proposals but takes no position on sovereignty.

- Qatar is wary that Iran might seek to encroach on its large North Field (natural gas), which it shares with Iran (the Iranian side is called South Pars). The North field is in operation and produces natural gas for export; Iran is developing its side of the field as well. Qatar's fears were heightened on April 26, 2004, when Iran's deputy Oil Minister said that Qatar is probably producing more gas than "her right share" from the field and that Iran "will not allow" its wealth to be used by others.

- In 1981 and again in 1996, Bahrain officially and publicly accused Iran of supporting Bahraini Shiite dissidents (the Islamic Front for the Liberation of Bahrain, Bahrain-Hizbollah, and other Bahraini dissident groups) in efforts to overthrow the ruling Al Khalifa family. Bahrain is about 60% Shiite, but its government is dominated by the Al Khalifa and other Sunni associates. Tensions have eased substantially during Khatemi's presidency, but Bahraini leaders remain wary that Tehran might again support Shiite unrest that rocked Bahrain during 1994-1998.

Iraq

The U.S. military ousting of Saddam Hussein appears to have benefitted Iran strategically. Iran publicly opposed the major U.S. military offensive against Iraq on the grounds that it was not authorized by the United Nations, but many observers believe Iran wanted Saddam

Hussein (a Sunni Muslim) removed, and the way cleared for the ascendancy of Iraq's Shiites to power in Iraq.[30] The main thrust of Iran's strategy in Iraq has been to persuade all Shiite Islamist factions in Iraq to work together to ensure Shiite Muslim dominance of post-Saddam Iraq. That strategy appears to have borne fruit with victory a Shiite Islamist bloc ("United Iraqi Alliance") in the January 30, 2005 National Assembly elections in Iraq. That bloc, which won 140 of the 275 Assembly seats, includes all of Iran's proteges in Iraq — the well-organized Shiite Islamist parties that Iran has supported since its 1979 Islamic revolution. The most pro-Iranian of these parties are the Supreme Council for the Islamic Revolution in Iraq (SCIRI), and, to a lesser extent, the Da'wa (Islamic Call) party. SCIRI was headed by Ayatollah Mohammad Baqr al-Hakim, the late Ayatollah Khomeini's choice to head an Islamic republic in Iraq, who returned to Iraq on May 10, 2003. He was killed in a car bombing in Najaf on August 29, 2003, and was succeeded by his younger brother, Abd al-Aziz al-Hakim. The new Prime Minister of Iraq is Da'wa's leader Ibrahim al-Jafari. Iranian leaders have also cultivated ties to Grand Ayatollah Ali al-Sistani, the 75-year-old Iranian-born Shiite cleric who is de-facto leader of the mainstream Shiite political bloc. However, Sistani has differed with Iran's doctrine of direct clerical involvement in government. The leading figures in the Iraqi Shiite bloc have said they will not seek to establish an Iranian-style theocratic regime, although some of them have said Islam should be a major factor in post-Saddam Iraq.

Iran showcased its growing influence in Iraq with a three-day visit (May 17-19, 2005) by Iranian Foreign Minister Kamal Kharrazi. During the visit, he met not only with Prime Minister Jafari but also with Grand Ayatollah Ali al-Sistani (see below) and Hakim. At the end of the visit, the two countries issued a joint communique in which Iraq essentially took responsibility for starting the 1980-1988 Iran-Iraq war and indirectly blamed Saddam Hussein for ordering the use of chemical weapons against Iranian forces during that conflict. The joint statement also condemned Israel and said Iran would open new consulates in Basra and Karbala (two major cities in Iraq's mostly Shiite south).

U.S. officials cite Iran for more ominous interference in Iraq. On September 8, 2004, Secretary of Defense Rumsfeld accused Iran of sending money and fighters to proteges in Iraq,[31] an assertion reiterated by CIA Director Porter Goss in March 17, 2005 testimony before the Senate Armed Services Committee. U.S. officials have declined to contradict speculation that Iran is also giving some backing (money and possibly arms and tactical military advice) to Shiite cleric Moqtada al-Sadr, whose "Mahdi Army" militia staged two major uprisings against U.S. and Iraqi forces (April and August 2004).[32] Most Iranian officials have sought to persuade Sadr to enter the legitimate political process, but some Iranian hardliners are said to prefer Sadr as a more anti-U.S. Shiite alternative in Iraq. Iran reportedly might be using its influence in Iraq to develop sources of information on U.S. operations in Iraq. Press reports say Iraqi political leader Ahmad Chalabi gave his Iranian contacts information on U.S. acquisition of Iranian intelligence codes.[33] Chalabi has denied the allegations.

Some Iranian conventional military moves at the border could reflect Iranian opposition to U.S.-led coalition operations in Iraq. On June 21, 2004, Iran seized eight British seamen on a mission in the waterway between Iran and southern Iraq. Iran released the British personnel after a few days' detention, although Britain says Iran had steered the British personnel into Iranian waters. Other minor altercations have occurred with Australian forces, and Iranian naval elements have sometimes crossed into Iraqi waters, according to U.S. military officials in the Persian Gulf.[34]

Some commentators say Iran will not exercise substantial influence in Iraq over the long term. They note that most Iraqi Shiites generally stayed loyal to the Iraqi regime during the 1980-1988 Iran-Iraq war, which took nearly 1 million Iranian lives and about half that many Iraqi battlefield deaths. Most Iraqi Shiites appear not to want a cleric-run Islamic regime. In addition, Iran and Iraq were not able to erase their bitterness from the Iran-Iraq war, despite completing exchanges of prisoners and remains from that war and despite an October 2000 agreement to abide by the waterway-sharing and other provisions of their 1975 Algiers Accords. (Iraq abrogated that agreement prior to its September 1980 invasion of Iran.) Iran has not returned the military and civilian aircraft flown to Iran at the start of the 1991 Gulf war, even though post-Saddam Iraqi politicians have said they want the aircraft returned. During the 1990s, Iran's naval forces did sometimes cooperate with Saddam Hussein's illicit export of oil through the Gulf, in exchange for substantial "protection fees."

Supporting Anti-Peace Process Groups

Many of the U.S. concerns about Iran's support for terrorism center on its reported material assistance (funds, advice, and some weaponry) to groups opposed to the Arab-Israeli peace process, the groups cited as receiving Iranian assistance by the April 2005 State Department report on terrorism (see above). U.S. State Department terrorism reports since 2002 have said that Iran has been encouraging coordination among Palestinian terrorist groups, particularly Hamas and PIJ, since the September 2000 Palestinian uprising. Iran also has sometimes openly incited anti-Israel violence, including hosting conferences of anti-peace process organizations (April 24, 2001, and June 2-3, 2002). In January 2002, according to U.S. and Israeli officials, Iran made a shipment, intercepted by Israel, of 50 tons of arms bought by the Palestinian Authority (PA). This action surprised many observers because Iran has traditionally had few ties to the non-Islamist Palestinian organizations.

On the other hand, there appear to be differences within Iran's leadership on Iran's policy toward the peace process. Khamene'i has continued to call Israel a "cancerous tumor" and make other statements suggesting that he seeks Israel's destruction. Khatemi, while publicly pledging support for the anti-peace process groups, sometimes tried to moderate Iran's position somewhat. The position of the Iranian Foreign Ministry, considered an institutional ally of reformists, is that Iran would not seek to block any final, two-state Israeli-Palestinian settlement.

Iran severed ties to Egypt after that country's 1979 peace treaty with Israel. In January 2004, Iran said it was close to agreement to restore full diplomatic ties with Egypt, and that it was going to meet an Egyptian demand to rename a Tehran street that is named after Khalid Islambouli, lead assassin of Anwar as-Sadat. However, diplomatic relations have not been restored to date.

Lebanese Hizballah

Iran maintains a close relationship with Lebanese Hizballah, a Shiite Islamist group, formed in 1982 by Lebanese Shiite clerics sympathetic to Iran's Islamic revolution and responsible for several acts of anti-U.S. and anti-Israel terrorism in the 1980s and 1990s.[35] There have been several press reports in 2004 and 2005 that Hizballah is assisting Hamas and PIJ plan attacks in Israel, even though Hizballah's main focus is on Lebanon. Hizballah maintains military forces along the border and operates outside Lebanese government control, even though the United Nations has certified that Israel had completed its withdrawal from southern Lebanon (May 2000). Hizballah asserts the withdrawal was incomplete and that Israel still occupies small tracts of Lebanese territory (Shebaa Farms). A small number (less than 50, according to a *Washington Post* report of April 13, 2005) of Iranian Revolutionary Guards reportedly remain in Lebanon to coordinate Iranian arms deliveries to Hizballah; the arms are offloaded in Damascus and trucked into Lebanon.[36] The reported shipments have included Stingers obtained by Iran in Afghanistan, mortars that can reach the Israeli city of Haifa if fired from southern Lebanon, and, in 2002, over 8,000 Katyusha rockets, according to Israeli leaders.[37] The State Department report on terrorism for 2004 (released April 2005) says Iran supplied Hizballah with the unmanned aerial vehicle (UAV), called the *Mirsad*, that Hizballah briefly flew over the border with Israel on November 7, 2004 (and on April 11, 2005).

Although Hizballah refuses to give up its militia force, a move required by U.N. Security Council Resolution 1559, it apparently is evolving into more of a political movement in Lebanon. In March 2005, Hizballah organized a huge demonstration against U.S. and other international pressure on Syria to completely withdraw from Lebanon, although Syria did subsequently withdraw its military (and intelligence) forces. After the completion of Lebanese parliamentary elections during May - June 2005, Hizballah has expanded its presence in the Lebanese parliament; it and its ally, the Shiite movement Amal, now hold 35 total seats in the 128-seat parliament. This positions Hizballah it to exert greater influence on Lebanese government decisions and to resist disarmament. Despite Hizballah's record of attacks on U.S. forces and citizens in Lebanon during the 1980s, President Bush indicated, in comments to journalists in March 2005, that the United States might accept Hizballah as a legitimate political force in Lebanon. In the 109th Congress, two similar resolutions (H.Res. 101 and S.Res. 82) have passed their respective chamber. The resolutions urge the EU to classify Hizballah as a terrorist organization and call on Hizballah to disband its militia as called for in U.N. Security Council Resolution 1559 (September 2, 2004).

Relations with Central Asia and the Caspian

Iran's policy in Central Asia has thus far emphasized economic cooperation over Islamic ideology, although it has sometimes become assertive in the region, particularly against Azerbaijan. That country's population, like Iran's, is mostly Shiite Muslim, but Azerbaijan has been ruled by secular leaders. In early 1992, Iran led the drive to bring the Central Asian states and Azerbaijan into the Economic Cooperation Organization.[38] Iran reportedly hosts at least one anti-Azerbaijan guerrilla leader (Hasan Javadov). In July 2001, Iranian warships and combat aircraft threatened a British Petroleum (BP) ship on contract to Azerbaijan out of an area of the Caspian Iran considers its own. The United States called that action provocative, and it offered new border security aid and increased political support to Azerbaijan. Iran and Armenia, an adversary of Azerbaijan, agreed on expanded defense cooperation in early March 2002. Iran- Azerbaijan tensions eased somewhat in conjunction with the mid-May 2002 visit by Azerbaijan's then President Heydar Aliyev, but there was little evident progress on a bilateral division of their portions of the Caspian. Strains will likely increase now that the Baku-Tblisi-Ceyhan oil pipeline, intended to reduce Western dependence on Iranian oil, is set to begin operations (see below).

Afghanistan/Al Qaeda[39]

Iran long opposed the puritanical Sunni Muslim regime of the Taliban in Afghanistan on the grounds that it oppressed Shiite Muslim and other Persian-speaking minorities, and reportedly is seeking to exercise influence over post-Taliban Afghanistan. Iran tacitly supported the U.S.-led war on the Taliban and Al Qaeda by offering the United States search and rescue of any downed service-persons and the transshipment to Afghanistan of humanitarian assistance. Iran has since moved to restore Iran's traditional sway in western, central, and northern Afghanistan where Persian-speaking Afghans predominate. Iran has expressed major objections to the U.S. use of Shindand air base in western Afghanistan, fearing it is being used to conduct surveillance on Iran. U.S. aircraft began using the base in September 2004 in connection with the downfall of local Afghan strongman Ismail Khan, who was Herat province governor and who previously had controlled the base. Suggesting it wants good relations with Afghanistan's leadership, in March 2002, Iran expelled Gulbuddin Hikmatyar, a pro- Taliban, pro-Al Qaeda Afghan faction leader. Iran froze Hikmatyar's assets in Iran in January 2005.

Although 18,000 U.S. troops are in Afghanistan and the regime there is pro- U.S., Iran believes its strategic position in Afghanistan is a vast improvement to its adversarial relationship with the Taliban. Iran nearly launched a military attack against the Taliban in September 1998 after Taliban fighters captured and killed several Iranian diplomats based in northern Afghanistan, and it provided military aid to the anti-Taliban Northern Alliance coalition, made up of mostly Persian-speaking minority groups. Iran, along with the United States, Russia, and the countries bordering Afghanistan, attended U.N.-sponsored meetings in New York (the Six Plus Two group) to try to end the internal conflict in Afghanistan.

Iran is not a natural ally of Al Qaeda, largely on the grounds that Al Qaeda is an orthodox Sunni Muslim organization. However, U.S. officials have said since January 2002 that it is unclear whether Iran has arrested senior Al Qaeda operatives who are believed to be in Iran.[40] These figures are purported to include Al Qaeda spokesman Sulayman Abu Ghaith, top operative Sayf Al Adl, and Osama bin Laden's son, Saad.[41] On July 23, 2003, Iranian officials, for the first time, asserted Iran had "in custody" senior Al Qaeda figures but did not name them publicly. Some accounts say the operatives who are in Iran have been able to contact associates outside Iran;[42] assertions to this effect were made by U.S. officials after the May 12, 2003 bombings in Riyadh, Saudi Arabia against four expatriate housing complexes and believed perpetrated by Al Qaeda. U.S. officials called on Iran to fulfill its "international obligations in the global war on terrorism" by turning them over to their countries of origin for trial. Hardliners in Iran might want to support or protect Al Qaeda activists as leverage against the United States and its allies, and some reports say Iran might want to exchange them for a U.S. hand-over of People's Mojahedin activists under U.S. control in Iraq.

The 9/11 Commission report said several of the September 11 hijackers and other plotters, possibly with official help, might have transited Iran, but the report does not assert that the Iranian government cooperated with or knew about the plot. In response to reports of the 9/11 Commission's findings, President Bush said the United States would continue to investigate possible ties between Iran and Al Qaeda.

Chapter 2

U.S. POLICY RESPONSES AND LEGISLATION

The February 11, 1979, fall of the Shah of Iran, a key U.S. ally, opened a long rift in U.S.-Iranian relations, but there have been several periods since 1997 when a significant and sustained thawing appeared imminent. On November 4, 1979, radical "students" seized the U.S. Embassy in Tehran and held its diplomats hostage until minutes after President Reagan's inauguration on January 20, 1981. The United States broke relations with Iran on April 7, 1980, and the two countries had only limited official contact since.[43] U.S. policy throughout the 1980s featured a marked tilt toward Iraq in the 1980-88 Iran-Iraq war, including U.S. diplomatic attempts to block conventional arms sales to Iran, providing battlefield intelligence to Iraq,[44] and, during 1987-88, direct skirmishes with Iranian naval elements in the course of U.S. efforts to protect international oil shipments in the Gulf from Iranian attacks.

The end of the Iran-Iraq war in August 1988 appeared to lay the groundwork for a reduction in U.S.-Iran hostility. In his January 1989 inaugural speech, President George H.W. Bush said that, in relations with Iran, "goodwill begets goodwill," holding out the prospect for better relations if Iran helped obtain the release of U.S. hostages held by Hizballah in Lebanon. Iran reportedly did assist in obtaining the release of all U.S. and other Western hostages in Lebanon by December 1991, but no substantial thaw followed, possibly because Iran continued to back Hizballah and other groups opposed to the U.S.-sponsored Middle East peace process. That process was a top Administration priority following the October 1991 Madrid Conference bringing together leaders from Israel, Syria, Lebanon, Jordan, and the Palestinians.

Upon taking office in 1993, the Clinton Administration moved to further isolate Iran as part of a strategy of "dual containment" of Iran and Iraq. In 1995 and 1996, the Clinton Administration and Congress added sanctions on Iran in response to growing concerns about Iran's weapons of mass destruction, its support for terrorist groups, and its efforts to subvert the Arab-Israeli peace process. (For details on U.S. sanctions against Iran, see below.) The election of Khatemi in May 1997 precipitated a U.S. shift toward engagement; the Clinton Administration offered Iran official dialogue, with no substantive preconditions. In January 1998, Khatemi publicly agreed to increase "people-to-people" exchanges with the United States but ruled out direct talks.

In a June 1998 speech, then Secretary of State Albright stepped up the U.S. outreach effort by calling for mutual confidence building measures that could lead to a "road map" for normalization of relations. Encouraged by the reformist victory in Iran's March 2000 parliamentary elections, Secretary Albright gave another speech on March 17, 2000, acknowledging past U.S. meddling in Iran, announcing an easing of sanctions on some Iranian imports, and promising to work to resolve outstanding claims disputes. Iran called the steps insufficient to warrant direct dialogue. In September 2000 "Millenium Summit" meetings at the United Nations, Albright and President Clinton sent a positive signal to Iran by attending Khatemi's speeches.

BUSH ADMINISTRATION POLICY AND OPTIONS

Four months after the September 11, 2001 attacks, President Bush named Iran as part of an "axis of evil" in his January 2002 State of the Union message, even though there has been no evidence Iran was involved in those attacks. To date, the Bush Administration has continued the main thrust of Clinton Administration efforts to engage Iran while at the same time trying to limit Iran's strategic capabilities through economic sanctions. In President Bush's second term, Iran's stepped up nuclear activity has stimulated consideration within the Administration of new options: pressuring Iran economically and diplomatically, acting against it directly including possibly militarily, promote a change of regime, or undertaking diplomatic engagement.

Regime Change

Some U.S. officials believe that only an outright change of regime would reduce substantially the strategic threat from Iran, because the current regime harbors ambitions fundamentally at odds with the United States and its values. Many question the prospects of success for this option, short of all-out-U.S. military invasion, because of the weakness of opposition groups committed to overthrowing Iran's regime. Providing overt or covert support to anti-regime organizations, in the view of many experts, would not make them materially more viable or attractive to Iranians. There has been some support in the United States for regime change since the 1979 Islamic revolution; the United States provided some funding to anti-regime groups, mainly pro-monarchists, during the 1980s.[45]

The United States has sought to promote U.S. values in Iran through broadcasting. Radio Free Europe/Radio Liberty (RFE/RL) has operated a radio service, in Farsi, to Iran since October 1998, broadcasting from Prague.[46] As of December 2002, it has been called Radio Farda ("Tomorrow" in Farsi), which now broadcasts 24 hours per day, at a cost of approximately $18 million per year. A U.S.- sponsored television broadcast service to Iran, run by the Voice of America (VOA), began operations on July 3, 2003. In early 2005, the VOA announced it is increasing the duration of the television broadcasts to three hours a day from 30 minutes a day.

The Bush Administration has shown substantial attraction to the regime change option since the September 11, 2001 attacks. On July 12, 2002, President Bush issued a statement supporting those Iranians demonstrating for reform and democracy, a message he reiterated on December 20, 2002, when he inaugurated Radio *Farda*. The statements appeared to signal a shift in U.S. policy from attempting to engage and support Khatemi to publicly supporting Iranian reformers and activists. On the other hand, as a sign of continued Administration hesitation on this option, on October 28, 2003, then Deputy Secretary of State

Armitage testified before the Senate Foreign Relations Committee that
the United States "does not have a regime change policy toward Iran."

President Bush's inaugural address (January 20, 2005) and his State
of the Union message (February 2, 2005) suggested that the
Administration, in its second term, would take further steps toward this
option, even as it backs European diplomacy with Iran on nuclear issues.
In the State of the Union message, he said "And to the Iranian people, I
say tonight: as you stand for your own liberty, America stands with you."
On her visit to Europe in early February 2005, Secretary of State Rice
said "I don't think that the unelected mullahs who run that regime are a
good thing for the Iranian people or for the region." On May 19, 2005,
Undersecretary of State for Political Affairs Nicholas Burns testified
before the Senate Foreign Relations Committee that "The United States
believes the future of Iran should be democratic and pluralistic. We
support those who wish to see Iran transformed from a rigid, intolerant
theocracy to a modern state ... We believe Iran is a country in the process
of change."

Some new options to promote regime change said to be under
consideration include increasing public criticism of the regime's human
rights record, and supporting Iranian dissidents.[47] An issue is whether
such democracy promotion efforts would be interpreted within Iran as
U.S. meddling — a sensitive issue in Iran, because the 1981 "Algiers
Accords" that settled the Iran hostage crisis provide for non-interference
in each others' internal affairs — and whether these programs would
reach sufficient numbers of Iranians to be effective.

The State Department has begun U.S. democracy promotion efforts
in Iran, using funds provided in recent appropriations, as discussed in the
State Department report "Supporting Human Rights and Democracy:
U.S. Record 2004-2005," released March 28, 2005). The following has
been appropriated:

- The FY2004 foreign operations appropriation (P.L. 108-199)
  earmarked "notwithstanding any other provision of law" up to
  $1.5 million for "making grants to educational, humanitarian and
  nongovernmental organizations and individuals inside Iran to
  support the advancement of democracy and human rights in
  Iran." The State Department Bureau of Democracy and Labor
  (DRL)[48] has given $1 million of those funds to a U.S.-based

organization, the Iran Human Rights Documentation Center, to document abuses in Iran, using contacts with Iranians in Iran. The Documentation Center is run mostly by persons of Iranian origin and affiliated with Yale University's "Griffin Center for Health and Human Rights." The remaining $500,000 is being distributed through the National Endowment for Democracy (NED).

- The conference report on H.R. 4818, (P.L. 108-447) the FY2005 foreign aid appropriations, provided a further $3 million for similar democracy promotion efforts in Iran using FY2005 funds. The State Department has put out a solicitation for proposals for similar projects to be funded in 2005. The solicitation closed on May 18, and DRL says that priority areas for grant awards are political party development, media development, labor rights, civil society promotion, and promotion of respect for human rights. DRL officials say they might fund exile broadcasting, as long as such broadcasting is not affiliated with an Iranian exile political faction.[49]

- The House version of the FY2006 foreign aid appropriation (H.R. 3057), as reported to the full House, would appropriate another $1.5 million in democracy promotion funds for use in Iran (and Syria).

Some in Congress are articulating a clear preference for further democracy promotion/regime change efforts toward Iran. In the 108th Congress, several bills (S. 1082, H.R. 2466, H.R. 5193) called for regime change and proposed to authorize funds to assist pro-democracy groups in Iran. In the 109th Congress, a provision of H.R. 2601, the State Department authorization bill marked up by the House International Relations Committee on June 8, 2005 states that it is the policy of the United States to support full democracy in Iran and the right of Iranian citizens to choose their system of government.

H.R. 282 and S. 333

Two major stand-alone bills in the 109th Congress represent this trend. H.R. 282, introduced by Representative Ros-Lehtinen, was marked up by the Middle East/Central Asia Subcommittee of the House

International Relations Committee on April 13, 2005. It has over 280 co-sponsors as of June 27, 2005, but the Administration reportedly views it as potentially complicating the EU nuclear talks with Iran. A similar bill, S. 333, has been introduced by Senator Santorum. These bills provide for the following.

- Both bills contain provisions increasing U.S. sanctions contained in the Iran-Libya Sanctions Act (ILSA), as discussed below and in CRS Report RS20871 on ILSA.
- Both recommend the appointment of an Administration policy coordinator on Iran, serving as a special assistant to the President.
- Both specify criteria for designating pro-democracy groups eligible to receive U.S. aid. S. 333 authorizes $10 million in U.S. funding for such groups; H.R. 282 authorizes no specific dollar amount.
- H.R. 282, as marked up by the House subcommittee, requires the Administration to work to secure a Security Council resolution requiring Iran to accept intrusive IAEA nuclear inspections.
- H.R. 282 calls for expanded U.S. contacts with groups attempting to promote democracy in Iran.
- Both call for Iranian government representatives to be denied access to all U.S. government buildings.

Engagement?

The Bush Administration has pursued engagement with Iran at times, although Administration discussion of this policy option has receded in 2005. Some U.S. officials have long believed that a policy of engagement would be more successful in curbing Iran's nuclear program and support for terrorist groups. In May 2003, both countries publicly acknowledged that they were conducting direct talks in Geneva on Afghanistan and Iraq,[50] marking the first confirmed direct dialogue between the two countries since the 1979 revolution. However, the United States broke off the dialogue following the May 12, 2003, bombing in Riyadh that U.S. officials say was planned by Al Qaeda activists in Iran. In December 2003, the United States resumed some contacts with Iran to coordinate U.S. aid to victims of the December 2003 earthquake in Bam, Iran, including a reported offer to send a high-level delegation to Iran, headed by Senator Elizabeth Dole and a Bush family member. (See further below.) However, Iran rebuffed the offer of the Dole mission. The Administration says it does not rule out future talks with Iran. Two late 2004 research institute reports, one by the Council on Foreign Relations and one by the Atlantic Council, recommended further pursuit of an engagement strategy with Iran, arguing that engagement could help promote regional stability and progress on issues in which there is U.S.-Iran agreement.[51]

The Administration appeared to support tentative moves by other governments and other branches of the U.S. government toward renewed engagement in 2004. In October-November 2004, Librarian of Congress James Billington visited Iran. The Bush Administration was informed in advance by the Librarian of his visit and said it viewed the visit as a cultural exchange consistent with U.S. policy. The main purpose of his visit was to begin an exchange of materials with Iran's national library and included cultural meetings with Iranian film experts, poets, and architects.

Military Action?

As concerns over Iran's nuclear program have grown, public discussion of a military option (conducted either by the United States or another country, such as Israel) against Iran's nuclear facilities has increased. Among outside experts, there has been speculation since the U.S.-led war against Iraq (begun March 19, 2003) that the United States might undertake major military action against other perceived threats such as Iran or Syria. However, all-out U.S. military action to remove Iran's regime appears to be unlikely and not under serious consideration by the Administration, although journalist Seymour Hersh reported that there is planning for such an attack, should the President order such action.[52] Most experts believe U.S. forces are likely spread too thin, including about 150,000 deployed in Iraq, to undertake it at this time and that U.S. forces would be greeted with hostility by most Iranians. At the same time, U.S. Central Command is updating its "war plan" for Iran, according to the *Washington Post* (February 10, 2005), as part of what

CENTCOM says is normal updating. A provision of the House-passed H.R. 1815, the FY2006 defense authorization bill, requires a Defense Department report to Congress on how the United States might be affected strategically and how it might respond to the acquisition by Iran of a nuclear weapon.

Some experts believe that limited military action, such as air strikes against suspected nuclear sites, could be a potentially useful option to set back Iran's nuclear program. On February 22, 2005, during his visit to Europe, President Bush attempted to calm European concerns about a possible U.S. strike on Iran, saying that "This notion that the United States is getting ready to attack Iran is simply ridiculous," but he counterbalanced that statement by saying that "all options are on the table."[53] On November 5, 2004, British Foreign Secretary Jack Straw said the United Kingdom could not see a circumstance that would allow it to support such an air strike by the United States, Israel, or any other force, on Iran at this time.

Some believe Iran might retaliate through terrorism or other means, and others question whether the United States is aware of all relevant sites. Still others maintain that Iran might have shielded some of its nuclear infrastructure from a strike. The January 2005 *New Yorker* piece by Seymour Hersh, referenced above, asserts that President Bush has authorized covert special forces missions into Iran to assess potential nuclear-related targets for a U.S. air strike. The Department of Defense criticized the credibility of the article, but it did not dispute this particular fact or other specific facts in it. In February 2005, there were press reports that the United States is flying unmanned aerial surveillance craft over Iran, in part to help survey nuclear sites, and as part of a broader U.S. review of its intelligence on Iran.[54]

Expressing particular fear that Iran might achieve a nuclear weapons capability, some Israeli officials, including Defense Minister Shaul Mofaz in October 2004, have openly refused to rule out the possibility that Israel might strike Iran's nuclear infrastructure, although Israel does not necessarily have the capabilities that the United States possesses that could conceivably make such action effective. On January 20, 2005, Vice President Cheney gave a radio interview suggesting that Israel might decide to undertake such a strike if the United States did not do so first. Israeli Prime Minister Ariel Sharon discussed the Iran nuclear issue with journalists and reportedly stressed with President Bush that Israel views the issue as an urgent and vital threat during his April 2005 visit to the United States. However, Sharon publicly said that Israel is not planning a military strike on Iran's facilities. Nonetheless, a Defense Department decision to sell Israel $30 billion worth of GBU- 28 "bunker buster" munitions has led to speculation that Israel might be contemplating such a strike, and with some degree of U.S. support.[55]

U.S. military analysts note that U.S. forces in the Gulf region could potentially be used against Iran, if the President so decides. Related options, which might involve U.S. naval forces in the Gulf, would be to institute searches of Iran-bound vessels suspected of containing WMD-related technology, or placing nuclear-armed weapons aboard U.S. ships operating in the Gulf as a signal of strength to Iran. The Administration has discussed with its allies some measures that could be used to block North Korea's technology exports and alleged drug smuggling,[56] an initiative that has won allied support. In contrast, some officials of allied governments, including Britain, have called for greater cooperation with Iran to curb the movement of smugglers and terrorists across the Persian Gulf.[57]

International Sanctions?

Iran is not subject to U.N. sanctions. However, during her visit to Europe in February 2005, Secretary of State Rice said that the Bush Administration believes that the EU-3 should agree with the United States that Iran should be reported to the Security Council, presumably for the imposition of sanctions, if it fails to uphold any aspect of its new nuclear pledges. At the same time, as noted above, in March 2005 the Administration decided to support the talks by offering to drop some U.S. sanctions on Iran (ending U.S. opposition to Iran's applying to join the WTO, and agreeing to sales of aircraft parts to Iran). During his February 2005 visit to Europe, several European leaders reportedly told the President that such a U.S. offer might help the prospects for achieving a permanent agreement. Under Secretary of State Burns testified before the Senate Foreign Relations Committee on May 19, 2005, that the Administration is not, at this point, considering any new incentives to support the EU-3 talks with Iran.

If further international sanctions are considered, some options that have been used or considered in similar cases could include the following.

- Imposing an international ban or limitations on purchases of Iranian oil or other trade. This sanction was imposed on Iraq after its 1990 invasion of Kuwait. However, this sanction is considered unlikely because world oil prices have risen to about $50 per barrel.

- Imposing an intrusive U.N.-led WMD inspections regime, similar to that imposed on Iraq after its defeat in the 1991 Persian Gulf war. The objective of such an inspections program, for example, could be to enforce a Security Council decision to prevent Iran from enriching uranium. Some might argue that the effectiveness of such a program might depend on the degree of Iranian cooperation with it.

- Imposing a worldwide ban on investment in Iran's energy sector, possibly to include construction of oil or gas pipeline linkages with Iran. This option could receive Security Council opposition on the same grounds as the oil purchase ban discussed above.

- Mandating reductions in diplomatic exchanges with Iran. This sanction was imposed on the Taliban government of Afghanistan in 1999 in response to its harboring of Al Qaeda leadership.

- Banning international flights to and from Iran. This sanction was imposed on Libya in response to the finding that its agents were responsible for the December 21, 1988, bombing of Pan Am 103.

- limiting further lending to Iran by international financial institutions.

Congress has approved legislation supporting international sanctions (and other measures) to prevent Iran from becoming a nuclear states. In the 108th Congress, a resolution, H.Con.Res. 398, passed the House on May 6, 2004, by a vote of 376-13. It called for the international community to use "all appropriate means to deter, dissuade, and prevent Iran from acquiring nuclear weapons, including ending all nuclear and other cooperation with Iran...." In the 109th Congress, a provision of a House-passed U.N. reform bill (H.R. 2745) calls on the United States to vote to ban the provision of peaceful nuclear technology to Iran unless the President certifies Iran is not enriching uranium (or committing other NPT violations).

U.S. SANCTIONS

Since the November 4, 1979, seizure of the U.S. hostages in Tehran, unilateral U.S. economic sanctions have formed a major part of U.S. policy toward Iran.[58] To date, few, if any, other countries have followed the U.S. lead by imposing sanctions on Iran, and no U.N. sanctions exist on that country. Some experts believe that U.S. sanctions have hindered Iran's economy, forcing it to curb spending on conventional arms purchases, but others believe that because the sanctions are not multilateral, the U.S. sanctions have had only marginal effect, and that foreign investment has flowed in nonetheless.[59] Those who take the latter view maintain that Iran's economic performance fluctuates according to the price of oil, and far less so from other factors. Because oil prices remain relatively high (nearly $60 per barrel), Iran's economy is growing about 5% per year. Iran's per capita income is estimated to now exceed $2,000 per year, up from about $1,700 in 2002.

Terrorism/Foreign Aid Sanctions

In January 1984, following the October 1983 bombing of the U.S. Marine barracks in Lebanon, believed perpetrated by Hizballah, Iran was added to the so-called "terrorism list." The terrorism list was established by Section 6(j) of the Export Administration Act of 1979, imposing economic sanctions on countries determined to have provided repeated support for acts of international terrorism. The designation bans direct U.S. financial assistance and arms sales, restricts sales of U.S. dual use items, and requires the United States to oppose multilateral lending to the designated countries. Separate from its position on the terrorism list, successive foreign aid appropriations laws since the late 1980s ban direct assistance to Iran (loans, credits, insurance, Eximbank credits) and indirect assistance (U.S. contributions to international organizations that work in Iran). Section 307 of the Foreign Assistance Act of 1961 (added in 1985) names Iran as unable to benefit from U.S. contributions to international organizations, and require proportionate cuts if these institutions work in Iran. Iran also has been designated every year since 1997 as not cooperating with U.S. anti-terrorism efforts, under the Anti-Terrorism and Effective Death Penalty Act (P.L. 104-132). That act penalizes countries that assist or sell arms to terrorism list countries.

U.S. regulations do not bar disaster relief and the United States donated $125,000, through relief agencies, to help victims of two earthquakes in Iran (February and May 1997), and another $350,000 worth of aid to the victims of a June 22, 2002 earthquake. (The World Bank provided some earthquake related lending as well, as discussed below.)

Bam Earthquake

The United States provided $5.7 million in assistance (out of total governmental pledges of about $32 million, of which $17 million have been remitted) to the victims of the December 2003 earthquake in Bam, Iran, which killed as many as 40,000 people and destroyed 90% of Bam's buildings. The United States flew in 68,000 kilograms of supplies to Bam, flown in by U.S. military flights, the first U.S. military flights into Iran since the abortive "Iran-Contra Affair" of 1985- 1986. The United States also deployed to Iran an 81-member Disaster Assistance Response Team (DART) composed of 7 USAID experts, 11 members of the Fairfax County (VA) urban search and rescue team, and 66 medical experts from the Federal Emergency Management Agency (FEMA). Iranian-American and other organizations coordinated donations in the United States for victims of the quake. On December 27, 2003, the Administration issued a 90-day amendment to the Iranian Transaction Regulations to authorize U.S. persons to make donations of funds for humanitarian relief for the earthquake victims. Under the amendment, Iranian-owned banks could be used to effect the transfer of funds, although no Iranian financing could be accessed.

Proliferation Sanctions

Several sanctions laws are unique to Iran. The Iran-Iraq Arms Nonproliferation Act (P.L. 102-484) requires denial of license applications for exports to Iran of dual use items, and imposes sanctions on foreign countries that transfer to Iran "destabilizing numbers and types of conventional weapons," as well as WMD technology. The Iran Nonproliferation Act (INA, P.L. 106-178) authorizes sanctions on foreign entities that assist Iran's WMD programs. [60] It bans U.S. extraordinary payments to the Russian Aviation and Space Agency in connection with the international space station unless the President can certify that the agency or entities under the Agency's control had not transferred any WMD or missile-related technology to Iran within the year prior. The provision contains certain exceptions to ensure the safety of astronauts who will use the international space station and for certain space station hardware. Unless the Administration determines that Russian entities are no longer violating the act, the provision could complicate U.S. efforts to keep U.S. astronauts on the station beyond April 2006, when Russia plans to start charging the United States for transporting them on its Soyuz spacecraft. The Administration, and NASA in particular, says it is looking for ways, consistent with the act, to continue to access the international space station.[61] A provision of the House-passed FY2006 defense authorization bill (H.R. 1815) expresses the sense of Congress that the INA not be "weakened" by creating exceptions to it that permit extraordinary payments to Russia.

Reflecting a Bush Administration decision to proceed with rather than overlook alleged violations or waive sanctions, the Bush Administration has sanctioned numerous entities, including from North Korea, China, India, Armenia, Taiwan, and Moldova. These entities were sanctioned under the INA, the Iran-Iraq Arms Non- Proliferation Act of 1992 (P.L. 102-484), and another law, the Chemical and Biological Warfare Elimination Act of 1991, for sales to Iran:

- In May 2003, the Bush Administration sanctioned a major Chinese industrial entity, Norinco, for allegedly selling missile technology to Iran.

- On July 4, 2003, an additional Chinese entity, the Taiwan Foreign Trade General Corporation, was sanctioned under the INA.

- On September 17, 2003, the Administration imposed sanctions on a leading Russian arms manufacturer, the Tula Instrument Design Bureau, for allegedly selling laser-guided artillery shells to Iran.

- On April 7, 2004, the Administration announced sanctions on 13 entities under the INA: Baranov Engine Building Association Overhaul Facility (Russia); Beijing Institute of Opto-Electronic Technology (China); Belvneshpromservice (Belarus); Blagoja Smakoski (Macedonia); Changgwang Sinyong Corp. (North Korea); Norinco (China); China Precision Machinery Import/Export Corporation (China); Elmstone Service and Trading (UAE); Goodly Industrial Co. (Taiwan); Mikrosam (Macedonia); Oriental Scientific Instruments Corp. (China); Vadim Vorobey (Russia); and Zibo Chemical Equipment Plant (China).

- In December 2004 and January 2005, INA sanctions were imposed on fourteen more entities, mostly from China, for alleged supplying of Iran's missile program. Many, such as North Korea's Changgwang Sinyong and China's Norinco and Great Wall Industry Corp, have been sanctioned several times previously. Other entities sanctioned included North Korea's Paeksan Associated Corporation, and Taiwan's Ecoma Enterprise Co.

The FY2005 foreign aid appropriation (P.L. 108-447) would punish the Russian Federation for assisting Iran. The law withholds 60% of any U.S. assistance to the Russian Federation unless it terminates technical assistance to Iran's civilian nuclear and ballistic missiles programs. Similar sanctions against
the Russian government for assisting Iran have been enacted in previous years, and the FY2006 foreign aid appropriation, as reported in the House, contains a similar provision.

Counter-Narcotics

In February 1987, Iran was first designated as a state that failed to cooperate with U.S. anti-drug efforts or take adequate steps to control narcotics production or trafficking. U.S. and U.N. Drug Control Program (UNDCP) assessments of drug production in Iran prompted the Clinton Administration, on December 7, 1998, to remove Iran from the U.S. list of major drug producing countries. The decision exempted Iran from the annual certification process that kept drug-related U.S. sanctions in place on Iran. According to several governments, over the past few years Iran has augmented security on its border with Afghanistan in part to prevent the flow of narcotics from that country into Iran. Britain has sold Iran night vision equipment and body armor for the counter-narcotics fight.

Trade Ban

On May 6, 1995, President Clinton issued Executive Order 12959 banning U.S. trade and investment in Iran. This followed an earlier March 1995 executive order barring U.S. investment in Iran's energy sector. The trade ban was partly intended to blunt criticism that U.S. trade with Iran made U.S. appeals for multilateral containment of Iran less credible. Each March since 1995, most recently on March 11, 2005, the U.S. Administration has renewed a declaration of a state of emergency that triggered the March 1995 investment ban. An August 1997 amendment to the trade ban (Executive Order 13059) prevented U.S. companies from knowingly exporting goods to a third country for incorporation into products destined for Iran. The following conditions and modifications apply.

- Some goods related to the safe operation of civilian aircraft may be licensed for export to Iran, and in December 1999, the Clinton Administration allowed the repair of engine mountings on seven Iran Air 747s (Boeing).
- Implementing regulations do not permit U.S. firms to negotiate investment deals with Iran or to trade Iranian oil overseas.
- Following a 1998 application by a U.S. firm to sell Iran agricultural products, and in the context of Clinton

Administration and congressional reviews of U.S. unilateral
sanctions policies, the Clinton Administration announced in
April 1999 that it would license, on a case-by-case basis,
commercial sales of food and medical products to certain
countries on which unilateral U.S. trade bans are in place (Iran,
Libya, and Sudan). Under regulations issued in July 1999,
private letters of credit can be used to finance approved sales,
but no U.S. government credit guarantees are available and U.S.
exporters are not permitted to deal directly with Iranian banks.
The FY2001 agriculture appropriations (P.L. 106-387) contained
a provision banning the use of official credit guarantees for food
and medical sales to Iran and other countries on the U.S.
terrorism list, except Cuba, although allowing for a presidential
waiver to permit such credit guarantees. Neither the Clinton
Administration nor the Bush Administration has provided the
credit guarantees. Iran says the lack of credit makes U.S. sales,
particularly of wheat, uncompetitive.

- After the March 2000 speech mentioned above, the trade ban
was eased to allow U.S. importation of Iranian nuts, dried fruits,
carpets, and caviar; regulations governing the imports were
issued in April 2000. The United States was the largest market
for Iranian carpets before the 1979 revolution, but U.S. anti-
dumping tariffs imposed on Iranian pistachio nut imports in
1986 (over 300%) dampened imports of that product. In January
2003, the tariff on roasted pistachios was lowered to 22% and on
raw pistachios to 163%. In December 2004, U.S. sanctions were
further modified to allow Americans to freely engage in ordinary
publishing activities with entities in Iran (and Cuba and Sudan).

- Subsidiaries of U.S. firms are not barred from dealing with Iran,
as long as the subsidiary has no operational relationship to the
parent company. Some U.S. companies have come under
scrutiny for dealings by their subsidiaries with Iran. On January
11, 2005, Iran said it had let a contract to the U.S. company
Halliburton, and an Iranian company, Oriental Kish, to drill for
gas in Phases 9 and 10 of South Pars. Under the deal,
Halliburton would reportedly provide its services, valued at $30
million to $35 million worth of fees per year, through Oriental
Kish. This leaves unclear whether Halliburton would be

considered in violation of the U.S. trade and investment ban, or ILSA.[62] Because of criticism within the United States, Halliburton announced on January 28, 2005, that it would withdraw all employees from Iran and end its pursuit of future business opportunities there, although it is not clear that Halliburton has pulled out of the Oriental Kish deal.[63] One week later, GE announced it would seek no new business in Iran. According to press reports, GE has been selling Iran equipment and services for hydroelectric, oil and gas services, and medical diagnostic projects through Italian, Canadian, and French subsidiaries. The trade ban appears to bar any Iranian company from buying a foreign company that has U.S. units.

The Iran-Libya Sanctions Act (ILSA) and Regional Oil and Gas Projects

A separate paper, CRS Report RS20871, *The Iran-Libya Sanctions Act*, assesses ILSA. ILSA (P.L. 104-172, August 5, 1996), as amended, sanctions foreign investment of more than $20 million in one year in Iran or Libya's energy sector. It was to sunset on August 5, 2001, but it was renewed for another five years (P.L. 107- 24, August 3, 2001). The renewal law required an Administration report on its effectiveness within 24-30 months, which did not recommend repeal. No sanctions have been imposed under ILSA, although three companies involved in one project (South Pars) were deemed in violation in September 1998; but sanctions were waived. A number of other investments have remained "under review" for ILSA sanctions since 1999. Those projects are discussed in CRS Report RS20871, mentioned above.

The U.S. trade ban permits U.S. companies to apply for licenses to conduct "swaps" of Caspian Sea oil with Iran, but, as part of a U.S. policy to route Central Asian energy around Iran (and Russia), a Mobil Corporation application to do so was denied in April 1999. The Bush Administration continues to oppose, and to threaten imposing ILSA sanctions on, regional pipeline projects that include Iran. U.S. policy promoted construction of a pipeline that would cross the Caspian Sea and terminate in Ceyhan, Turkey (Baku-Ceyhan pipeline); the policy appeared to bear fruit when four Caspian nations (Turkey, Georgia,

Azerbaijan, and Kazakhstan) formally embraced the route in November 1999. Regional and corporate support for the project subsequently gained momentum, construction began, and the pipeline has begun preliminary operations as of May 2005. On the other hand, despite U.S. pressure not to import Iranian gas, in December 2001 Turkey began doing so through a new cross-border pipeline, under an August 1996 agreement. On the other hand, Iran is said to be importing gasoline possibly from these or Persian Gulf state sources because of a lack of adequate refining capacity in Iran.

A major emerging issue is that of a proposed gas pipeline from Iran to India, through Pakistan, and with a possible extension to China. The idea is an outgrowth of the growing gas sales relationship with India. Leaders of Iran, Pakistan, and India all say they want to pursue the project, despite U.S. opposition, and India and Pakistan have formed a working group to accelerate the project. During her visit to Asia in March 2005, Secretary of State Rice "expressed U.S. concern" about the pipeline deal, although neither she nor any other U.S. official has directly stated that it would be reviewed for ILSA sanctions.[64] On June 7, 2005, U.S. Ambassador to Pakistan Ryan Crocker denied that the United States is pressuring Pakistan not to agree to the project.

As discussed above in the section on "regime change," H.R. 282 and S. 333 have several provisions to amend ILSA. These provisions are as follows:

- to increase the requirements on the Administration to justify waiving sanctions on companies determined to have violated its provisions;
- to repeal the sunset (expiration) provision of ILSA; and
- to make exports to Iran of WMD-useful technology sanctionable under ILSA.[65]

H.R 282, as marked up, also

- cuts U.S. assistance to countries whose companies have invested in Iran's energy sector;
- sets a 90-day time limit for the Administration to determine whether a company has violated ILSA's provisions; and

- requires public disclosure of investment funds that have investments in companies that have invested in Iran's energy sector. (Some of these disclosure provisions are contained in separate bills, H.R. 1743 and S. 299).

Travel-Related Guidance

Use of U.S. passports for travel to Iran is permitted, but a State Department travel warning, softened somewhat in April 1998, asks that Americans "defer" travel to Iran. Iranians entering the United States are required to be fingerprinted.

U.S. Iran Assets Disputes

Iran views the issue of outstanding disputed commercial claims and U.S.-blocked assets as an obstacle to improved relations. A U.S.-Iran Claims Tribunal at the Hague is arbitrating cases resulting from the break in relations and freezing of some of Iran's assets following the Iranian revolution. The major cases yet to be decided center on hundreds of Foreign Military Sales cases between the United States and the Shah's regime, which Iran claims it paid for but were unfulfilled. About $400 million in proceeds from the resale of that equipment is in a DOD account, and about $22 million in Iranian diplomatic property remains blocked. The assets issue moved to the forefront following several U.S. court judgments against Iran for past acts of terrorism against Americans, filed under the Anti-Terrorism and Effective Death Penalty Act of 1996.[66]

Regarding the mistaken U.S. shoot-down on July 3,1988 of an Iranian Airbus passenger jet, on February 22, 1996, the United States, responding to an Iranian case before the International Court of Justice (ICJ), agreed to pay Iran up to $61.8 million in compensation ($300,000 per wage earning victim, $150,000 per non wage earner) for the 248 Iranians killed. The funds for this settlement came from a general appropriation for judgments against the United States. The United States previously paid $3 million in death benefits for 47 non-Iranians killed in the attack, but has not compensated Iran for the airplane itself. A different case, pending before the ICJ, involves an Iranian claim for damages to Iranian oil platforms during U.S. naval clashes with Iran in October 1987 and April 1988.

MULTILATERAL POLICIES TOWARD IRAN

A cornerstone of the policies of successive U.S. administrations has been to persuade U.S. allies to cooperate with the United States to contain Iran, including imposing their own sanctions on that country. As noted, those U.S. efforts have generally been unsuccessful, because most U.S. allies see engagement as useful means of moderating Iran. During 1992-1997, the European Union (EU) countries maintained a policy of "critical dialogue" with Iran, asserting that dialogue and commerce with Iran could moderate Iran's behavior. The United States did not oppose those talks but maintained that the EU's dialogue would not change Iranian behavior. The dialogue was suspended immediately following the April 1997 German terrorism trial ("Mykonos trial") that found high-level Iranian involvement in assassinating Iranian dissidents in Germany. Alongside Khatemi's accession, the EU-Iran dialogue formally resumed in May 1998. He undertook state visits to several Western countries, including Italy (March 1999), France (October 1999), Germany (July 2000), and Japan (November 2000); the United States publicly welcomed these visits.

Eu-Iran Trade Negotiations

On December 12, 2002, Iran and the EU (European Commission) began negotiations on a "Trade and Cooperation Agreement" (TCA) that would lower the tariffs or increase quotas for Iranian exports to the EU countries, with linkage to Iran's addressing EU concerns on Iran's human rights practices and terrorism sponsorship. However, revelations about Iran's possible nuclear weapons ambitions caused the EU to suspend talks on a TCA in July 2003. As noted above, the EU - Iran TCA talks resumed in January 2005 in concert with negotiations on a permanent nuclear agreement. The EU has said a TCA depends on more than just nuclear issues, and the EU has insisted on working group discussions on

Iran's human rights record, Iran's alleged efforts to derail the Middle East peace process, Iran's record of supporting terrorism (Al Qaeda, Hezbollah, Hamas, and the PMOI, which Iran considers a terrorist group, although the EU does not), and proliferation issues. These working groups include discussions on counter-narcotics, refugees, and migration issues — issues on which Iran's record has sometimes been positive.

Country-Specific Policies: Britain and France

The 1998 resolution of the "Rushdie affair" to Britain's satisfaction sparked improvement in its relations with Iran. Iran maintains that Ayatollah Khomeini's 1989 death sentence against author Salman Rushdie cannot be revoked (his "Satanic Verses" novel was labeled blasphemous) because Khomeini is no longer alive to revoke it. On September 24, 1998, Iran's Foreign Minister pledged to Britain that Iran would not seek to implement the sentence and opposed any bounties offered for his death. Britain then upgraded relations with Iran to the ambassadorial level. Some Iranian clerics (outside the formal government structure) have said the death sentence stands, and the Iranian government has not required the Fifteen Khordad foundation to withdraw its $2.8 million reward for Rushdie's death. Khatemi said on June 4, 2001 that he considers the issue closed. In October 2000, Britain began extending longer term credit (two years or greater) for exports to Iran.

As noted above (ILSA section), French-Iranian economic relations have burgeoned in recent years. French investment in Iran now goes well beyond the energy sector into car production in Iran and other initiatives. Some of the major French companies investing in Iran (outside the energy sector) include Renault, Societe-Generale (banking), Peugeot, and Alcatel.

Japan/Azadegan Field

In August 1999, Japan continued a gradual improvement in relations with Iran by announcing a resumption of Japan's official development lending program for Iran to construct a hydroelectric dam over the Karun

River. However, the $70 million increment announced was less than Iran had wanted, and Japan said that this tranche would close out Japan's involvement in the project. (In 1993, Japan provided the first $400 million tranche of the overall $1.4 billion official development loan program, but the lending was subsequently placed on hold as the United States sought to persuade its allies to pressure Iran.) In late January 2000, Japan agreed to resume medium- and long-term export credit insurance for exports to Iran, suspended since 1994. Economic relations improved further during Khatemi's November 2000 visit to Tokyo, which resulted in Iran granting Japanese firms the first right to negotiate to develop the large Azadegan field. Partly at U.S. urging, Japan has refused to extend to Iran new official loans.

Multilateral and World Bank Lending to Iran

During 1994-1995, and over U.S. objections at the time, Iran's European and Japanese creditors rescheduled about $16 billion in Iranian debt. These countries (governments and private creditors) rescheduled the debt bilaterally, in spite of Paris Club rules that call for multilateral rescheduling and International Monetary Fund (IMF) involvement. Iran has worked its external debt down from $32 billion in 1997 to below $20 billion as of March 2004, according to Iran's Central Bank. The improved debt picture has led most European export credit agencies to restore insurance cover for exports to Iran. In July 2002, Iran tapped international capital markets for the first time since the Islamic revolution, selling $500 million in bonds to European banks. At the urging of the U.S. government, in May 2002 Moody's stopped its credit ratings service for Iran's government bonds on the grounds that performing the credit ratings service might violate the U.S. trade ban.

Section 1621 of the Anti-Terrorism and Effective Death Penalty Act of 1996 (P.L. 104-132) amended the Foreign Assistance Act to require the United States to vote against international loans to countries on the U.S. terrorism list. Acting under provisions of successive foreign aid laws, in 1993 the United States voted its 16.5% share of the World Bank against loans to Iran of $460 million for electricity, health, and irrigation projects. To signal opposition to international lending to Iran, the FY1994 foreign aid appropriations (P.L. 103-87) cut the

Administration's request for the U.S. contribution to the World Bank by the amount of those loans. That law, as well as the foreign aid appropriations for FY1995 (P.L. 103-306) and FY1996 (P.L. 104-107), would have significantly reduced U.S. payments to the Bank if it had provided new loans to Iran.

By 1999, Iran's moderating image had led the World Bank to consider new loans. U.S. policy, as explained on October 29, 2003, a Treasury Department official, Bill Schuerch, in testimony before the House Financial Services Committee, has been to try to block the World Bank loans to Iran. However, the United States does not have a large enough voting share to guarantee that outcome. In May 2000, the United States' allies outvoted the United States and approved $232 million in loans for health and sewage projects. In May 2001 the Bank approved a two-year economic reform plan for Iran that envisioned $775 million in new Bank loans. During April 2003 - May 2005, a total of $725 million in loans were approved for environmental management, housing reform, water and sanitation projects, and land management projects, in addition to a $400 million in loans for earthquake relief. (On July 15, 2004, a proposed amendment to the House version of the FY2005 foreign aid appropriations, H.R. 4818, was defeated. It would have cut U.S. funding to the World Bank by the $360 million in loans to Iran that the Bank had approved in May 2004.)

In 1999-2000, Iran had asked the International Monetary Fund for about $400 million in loans (its quota is about $2 billion) to help it deal with its trade financing shortfalls. However, Iran balked at accepting IMF conditionality, and there was no agreement.

WTO MEMBERSHIP

Iran first attempted to apply to join the WTO in July 1996. On 22 occasions after that, representatives of the Clinton and then the Bush Administration blocked Iran from applying (applications must be by consensus of the 148 members). As discussed above, as part of an effort to assist the EU-3 nuclear talks with Iran, the Administration announced on March 11, 2005, that it would drop opposition to Iran's applying for WTO membership if a nuclear deal is reached. In May 2005, when it appeared the EU-3 talks with Iran might collapse, the United States dropped its opposition to Iran's application, and Iran began accession talks. The talks could take many years, as Iran's economy contains some structural imbalances and restrictions, such as control of major economic sectors or markets by the quasi-statal "foundations" (*bonyads*), that would need to be reformed before Iran could obtain full membership.

Chapter 3

CONCLUSION

Mistrust between the United States and Iran's Islamic regime has run deep for over two decades. Many experts say that all factions in Iran are united on major national security issues and that U.S.-Iran relations might not improve unless or until the Islamic regime is removed or moderates substantially. Some believe that a crisis is likely if Iran does not fully and unambiguously abandon any efforts toward achieving a nuclear weapons capability.

Others say that, despite the victory of conservatives in 2004 parliamentary elections, the United States and Iran have a common interest in stability in the Persian Gulf and South Asia regions in the aftermath of the defeat of the Taliban and the regime of Saddam Hussein. Those who take this view say that Iran is far more secure now that the United States has removed these two regimes, and it might be more willing than previously to accommodate U.S. interests in the Gulf. Others say that the opposite is more likely, that Iran now feels more encircled than ever by pro- U.S. regimes and U.S. forces guided by a policy of pre-emption, and Iran might redouble its efforts to develop WMD and other capabilities to deter the United States.

REFERENCES

[1] The Council of Guardians consists of six Islamic jurists and six secular lawyers. The six Islamic jurists are appointed by the Supreme Leader. The six lawyers on the Council are selected by the Majles (parliament).

[2] Bush Criticizes Iran Election Process as Unfair. Reuters, June 16, 2005.

[3] Other names by which this group is known is the Mojahedin-e-Khalq Organization (MEK or MKO) and the National Council of Resistance (NCR).

[4] The designation was made under the authority of the Anti-Terrorism and Effective Death Penalty Act of 1996 (P.L. 104-132).

[5] "Removal of Iran Group From Terror List Sought." *Washington Post*, November 23, 2002.

[6] Cloud, David. "U.S., Iran Hit Bumpy Terrain on Road to Rapprochement." *Wall Street Journal*, May 12, 2003.

[7] For further information, see CRS Report RL31119, *Terrorism: Near Eastern Groups and State Sponsors, 2002*.

[8] Kampeas, Ron. (2002). "Iran's Crown Prince Plots Nonviolent Insurrection from Suburban Washington." *Associated Press*, August 26.

[9] For text of the 2004 report on Iran, see [http://www.state.gov/g/drl/rls/hrrpt/2004/ 41721.htm].

[10] Jacoby testimony before the Senate Intelligence Committee. February 16, 2005.

[11] For further information, see CRS Report RL30551, *Iran: Arms and Weapons of Mass Destruction Suppliers*.

[12] For further information, see CRS Report RS21592, *Iran's Nuclear Program: Recent Developments.*

[13] The Central Intelligence Agency, in an unclassified report to Congress covering July 1, 2003 - December 31, 2003, says the "United States remains convinced that Tehran has been pursuing a clandestine nuclear weapons program..."

[14] Weisman, Steven. (2005). "Sharon, Ending U.S. Visit, Says Israel Has No Plan to Hit Iran." *New York Times*, April 14.

[15] Lancaster, John and Kamran Khan. (2004). "Pakistanis Say Nuclear Scientists Aided Iran." *Washington Post*, January 24.

[16] Murphy, Francois. (2004). "U.N. Watchdog Accuses Iran of Unanswered Questions." *Reuters*, February 25.

[17] Nuclear experts say that could, in theory, be sufficient to yield as many as five nuclear bombs.

[18] Weisman, Steven. (2004). "U.S. In Talks With Europeans on a Nuclear Deal With Iran." *New York Times*, October 12.

[19] "Unclassified Report to Congress on the Acquisition of Technology Relating to Weapons of Mass Destruction and Advanced Conventional Munitions, 1 July Through 31 December 2003" [http://www.cia.gov].

[20] See CRS Report RS21548, *Iran's Ballistic Missile Capabilities.*

[21] Wright, Robin and Keith Richburg. (2004).Powell Says Iran is Pursuing Bomb. *Washington Post,* November 18.

[22] Jehl, Douglas. (2004). "Iran Reportedly Hides Work On a Longer-Range Missile," *New York Times*, December 2.

[23] "Greater U.S. Concern About Iran Missile Capability." *Reuters*, March 11, 2002.

[24] "Iran: New Missile on the Assembly Line." *New York Times*, September 26, 2002.

[25] U.S. Department of State. *Patterns of Global Terrorism:2002.* Released April 2003,

[26] Militant Recruiters Out in Open in Tehran. *Washington Times*, December 16, 2004.

[27] Kemp, Geoffrey. (1994). *Forever Enemies? American Policy and the Islamic Republic of Iran.* Carnegie Endowment for International Peace, pp. 82-88.

[28] See CRS Report RL31533, *The Persian Gulf States: Issues for U.S. Policy, 2004.*

[29] Walsh, Elsa. (2001). "Annals of Politics: Louis Freeh's Last Case." *The New Yorker*, May 14, The June 21, 2001 federal grand jury indictments of 14 suspects (13 Saudis and a Lebanese citizen) in the Khobar bombing indicate that Iranian agents may have been involved, but no indictments of any Iranians were announced. In June 2002, Saudi Arabia reportedly sentenced some of the eleven Saudi suspects held there. The 9/11 Commission final report asserts that Al Qaeda might have had some as yet undetermined involvement in the Khobar Towers attacks.

[30] "Iran's Kharrazi Hopes for Shiite Role in Iraq." *Reuters*, April 9, 2003.

[31] Scarborough, Rowan. (2004)."Rumsfeld: Iran Aids Rebels." *Washington Times*, September 8.

[32] Wong, Edward. (2004). "Iran Is In Strong Position to Steer Iraq's Political Future." *New York Times*, July 3.

[33] Risen, James and David Johnston. (2004). "Chalabi Reportedly Told Iran That U.S. Had Code." *New York Times*, June 2.

[34] CRS conversations with U.S. Fifth Fleet commander, Vice Admiral Nickels, in Bahrain, February 2005.

[35] Hizballah's last known terrorist attacks outside Lebanon was the July 18, 1994 bombing of a Jewish community center in Buenos Aires, which killed 85. On March 11, 2003, an Argentinian judge issued arrest warrants for four Iranian diplomats, including Intelligence Minister Ali Fallahian, for alleged complicity in the attack. Hizballah is also believed to have committed the March 17, 1992 bombing of Israel's embassy in that city.

[36] Wright, Robin. (2001). "U.S. Blocks A Key Iran Arms Route to Mideast." *Los Angeles Times*, May 6.

[37] "Israel's Peres Says Iran Arming Hizbollah." *Reuters*, February 4, 2002.

[38] The ECO was founded in 1985 by Iran, Pakistan, and Turkey, as a successor to an organization founded by those states in 1964.

[39] See CRS Report RL30588, *Afghanistan: Post-War Governance, Security, and U.S. Policy*.

[40] Keto, Alex. (2003). "White House Reiterates Iran Is Harboring Al Qaeda." *Dow Jones Newswires*, May 19.

[41] Gertz, Bill. (2003). "Al Qaeda Terrorists Being Held by Iran." *Washington Times*, July 24.

[42] Gertz, Bill. (2004)."CIA Points to Continuing Iran Tie to Al Qaeda." *Washington Times*, July 23.

[43] An exception was the abortive 1985-86 clandestine arms supply relationship with Iran in exchange for some American hostages held by Hizballah in Lebanon (the so-called "Iran-Contra Affair").

[44] Sciolino, Elaine. (1991). *The Outlaw State: Saddam Hussein's Quest for Power and the Gulf Crisis*. New York, USA: John Wiley and Sons, p.168.

[45] CRS conversations with U.S. officials responsible for Iran policy. 1980-1990. After a period of suspension of such assistance, in 1995, the Clinton Administration accepted a House-Senate conference agreement to include $18-$20 million in funding authority for covert operations against Iran in the FY1996 Intelligence Authorization Act (H.R. 1655, P.L. 104-93), according to a *Washington Post* report of December 22, 1995. The Clinton Administration reportedly focused the covert aid on changing the regime's behavior, rather than its overthrow.

[46] The service began when Congress funded it ($4 million) in the conference report on H.R. 2267 (H.Rept. 105-405), the FY1998 Commerce/State/ Justice appropriation. It was to be called "Radio Free Iran."

[47] Strobel, Warren. (2004). "U.S. Planning to Put More Pressure on Iran." *Miami Herald*, December 9.

[48] The State Department has determined that, because Iran is ineligible for U.S. aid, Iran democracy promotion funds cannot be channeled through the Middle East Partnership Initiative, because those are Economic Support Funds, ESF, and cannot be used in Iran.

[49] Briefing by DRL representatives for congressional staff. May 9, 2005.

[50] Wright, Robin. (2003)." U.S. In 'Useful' Talks With Iran." *Los Angeles Times*, May 13.

[51] For text of the Council on Foreign Relations study, see [http://www.cfr.org/pdf/Iran _TF.pdf].

[52] Hersh, Seymour. (2005). "The Coming Wars." *The New Yorker*, January 17.

[53] Fletcher, Michael and Keith Richburg. (2005). Bush Tries to Allay E.U. Worry Over Iran. *Washington Post*, February 23.

[54] Linzer, Dafna. (2005).U.S. Uses Drones to Probe Iran For Arms. *Washington Post*, February 13, 2005; Linzer, Dafna and Walter Pincus. U.S. Reviewing Its Intelligence on Iran. *Washington Post*, February 12.

[55] Stone, Andrea. (2005). "U.S. Plans to Sell 100 Bunker Busting Bombs to Israel." *USA Today*, April 18.

[56] Kralev, Thomas.(2003)."U.S. Asks Aid Barring Arms From Rogue States." *Washington Times*, June 5.

[57] "British Commander Calls for More Cooperation With Iran in Persian Gulf." *BBC*, May 3, 2004.

[58] On November 14, 1979, President Carter declared a national emergency with respect to Iran, renewed every year since 1979.

[59] "The Fight Over Letting Foreigners Into Iran's Oilfields." *The Economist*, July 14, 2001.

[60] See CRS Report RS22072, *The Iran Nonproliferation Act and the International Space Station: Issues and Options.* By Sharon Squassoni and Marcia Smith.

[61] Gugliotta, Guy. (2004). "Long Arm of Foreign Policy." *Washington Post*, August 25.

[62] "Iran Says Halliburton Won Drilling Contract." *Washington Times,* January 11, 2005.

[63] Boyd, Roderick.(2005).Halliburton Agrees to Leave Iran, Thompson Says. *New York Sun*, March 25.

[64] Some of the Indian companies that reportedly might take part in the pipeline project are: Oil and Natural Gas Corp. GAIL (India) Ltd. Indian Oil Corp. and Bharat Petroleum Corp. Some large European companies have also expressed interest. See, Solomon, Jay and Neil King. "U.S. Tries to Balance Encouraging India-Pakistan Rapprochement With Isolating Tehran." *Wall Street Journal*, June 24, 2005. P. A4.

[65] ILSA sanctions with respect to Libya were terminated on April 23, 2004, on the grounds that the President certified Libya had complied with U.N. Security Council resolutions related to the December 21, 1988, bombing of Pan Am Flight 103.

[66] See CRS Report RL31258, *Suits Against Terrorism States by Victims of Terrorism.*

INDEX